in

ENGINEERING

CAREERS in ENGINEERING

GERALDINE GARNER

THIRD EDITION

New York Chicago San Francisco Lisbon London Madrid Mexico City
Milan New Delhi San Juan Seoul Singapore Sydney Toronto

The **McGraw·Hill** Companies

Library of Congress Cataloging-in-Publication Data

Garner, Geraldine O.
    Careers in engineering / by Geraldine Garner.—3rd ed.
      p.   cm.
    ISBN 0-07-154555-7 (alk. paper)
    1. Engineering—Vocational guidance.   I. Title.

  TA157.G3267 2009
  620.0023'73—dc22   2008018216

1 2 3 4 5 6 7 8 9 10 11 12 13 14 15 16 17 18 19 20 21 DOC/DOC 0 9 8

ISBN 978-0-07-154555-6
MHID   0-07-154555-7

McGraw-Hill books are available at special quantity discounts to use as premiums and sales promotions or for use in corporate training programs. To contact a representative, please visit the Contact Us pages at www.mhprofessional.com.

This book is printed on acid-free paper.

This book is dedicated to Jerry.

CONTENTS

ACKNOWLEDGMENTS

This book would not have been possible without the invaluable contributions of organizations such as the American Society of Civil Engineering and the American Institute of Aeronautics and Astronautics, which contributed chapter content to assure accuracy and thoroughness. The book also benefits from the insights and expertise of people such as David Siegel of the National Society for Professional Engineers who made sure that the book contains the most up-to-date information on professional licensing for engineers. Leann Yoder, Executive Director, Junior Engineering Technical Society, has provided great tips on how to deal with the challenges of math and science so that they don't stand in your way of becoming a great engineer. Similarly, Melissa Tata, Senior Manager at Dell and member of the Board of the Society of Women Engineers, and Andrew Horn, Project Manager at The Rise Group, provided great insights and advice to women and minorities who are considering a career in engineering. Other contributors include Liz Glazer of ABET, Inc.; Veena Kumar, Bovis Lend Lease; John Fabijanic, California Polytechnic State University, San Luis Obispo; Greg Geiger, The American Ceramic Society; and Dwight Wardell, American Society for Engineering Education. They each have made this book better and stronger.

PART
ONE

Engineering:
The Career Field
That Improves Our
Quality of Life

CHAPTER

1

WHAT IS ENGINEERING?

In 1989, Dean Kamen, inventor of the Segway, founded a unique competition for high school students interested in science and engineering. It is called **FIRST**, which stands for For Inspiration and Recognition of Science and Technology. The mission of FIRST is to "inspire young people to be science and technology leaders, by engaging them in exciting mentor-based programs that build science, engineering and technology skills, that inspire innovation, and that foster well-rounded life capabilities including self-confidence, communication and leadership."

FIRST has had tremendous success in attracting growing numbers of high school students to the exciting field of engineering. In fact, the competition has grown so large that now the finals for the national FIRST competition are held in the Georgia Dome!

Programs like FIRST are very important in helping young people learn about the exciting possibilities of an engineering career and the skills needed. Despite the efforts of these programs, however, many young people still don't know what engineering is all about. In these pages, you will find information about engineering careers, programs like FIRST, and the steps needed to enter the field of engineering.

OVERVIEW OF ENGINEERING

The website discoverengineering.org says that engineering is the "stealth profession because most people have no idea what engineers do." If you are reading this book, either you know some of the things that engineers do or you are interested in learning what they do. In either case, this book will not only look at engineering, in general, but also at specific types of engineering. The goal is to show the many opportunities that exist for people who are interested in making our society better.

Are you a person who is interested in making society better? There are some ways to tell. Are you curious about how things work? Do you enjoy working on teams? Are you good at putting puzzles together? Do you like to solve problems? Do you think in a logical, well-organized fashion? Would you like to design or make things that improve people's lives? If you answered "yes" to any or all of these questions, keep reading because the field of engineering might offer you a very rewarding career.

The field of engineering has often been compared to both art and science. According to Henry Petroski, in *To Engineer Is Human*, "Engineering does share traits with both art and science, for engineering is a human endeavor that is both creative and analytical." However, engineering is neither science nor art. Engineers create solutions to human problems using the principles discovered by scientists and mathematicians.

It is often said that engineers are an extremely creative group of people! They are problem-solvers. They invent the things that we need, and they improve things that are not working well for us. Just look around you and you will see the creativity and beauty of engineers' work—from the Golden Gate Bridge in San Francisco to the space shuttle to high-tech operating rooms in today's hospitals. Engineering marvels touch our daily lives: iPods, high-definition televisions, personal digital assistants (PDAs), cell phones, convection and microwave ovens, snowblowers, jet skis, race cars, thermal coats, disposable cameras, compact hair dryers, frozen pizzas, the Internet! The list can and will go on and on as engineers continue to create and invent the solutions people need.

What is engineering? Many definitions have been written. The American Society of Engineering Education says, "Engineering is the profession in which a knowledge of the mathematical and natural sciences gained by study, experience, and practice is applied with judgment to develop ways to utilize the materials and forces of nature, economically for the benefit of mankind."

No matter which definition appeals to you, there is no mistake. Engineers are creative and they are problem-solvers who rely on the discoveries of math and science to improve the world in which we live. In his book, *Studying Engineering*, Raymond Landis, Dean of Engineering and Technology at California State University in Los Angeles, lists ten rewards of an engineering career:

1. Job satisfaction
2. Variety of career opportunities
3. Challenging work
4. Intellectual development
5. Potential to benefit society
6. Financial security
7. Prestige
8. Professional environment
9. Technological and scientific discovery
10. Creative thinking

If these rewards appeal to you, engineering might be the right career for you.

A HISTORY OF ENGINEERING

Having stated that engineers are creative problem-solvers, one could come to the conclusion that engineering is a new career field that has emerged as a result of the many inventions of the twentieth century that dramatically changed the way people live. While it is true that the field of engineering has changed and grown in recent years, engineering is an established career field with a long and distinguished history.

The first engineer known by name and achievement is Imhotep, who built the famous stepped pyramid in Egypt circa 2550 B.C. The Persians, Greeks, and Romans, along with the Egyptians, took engineering to remarkable heights by using arithmetic, geometry, and physical science. Many famous ancient structures that are still standing today demonstrate the ingenuity and skill of these early engineering pioneers.

Similar to these ancient engineers, Medieval European engineers combined military and civil skills to carry construction to heights unknown by those who had come before. They developed techniques known as the Gothic arch and flying buttress. The sketchbook of Villard de Honnecourt, who lived and worked in the early thirteenth century, demonstrates the Gothic engineer's remarkable knowledge of natural and physical science, mathematics, geometry, and draftsmanship.

In Japan, China, India, and other Far Eastern areas, engineering developed separately but similarly. The sophisticated techniques of construction, hydraulics, and metallurgy practiced in the Far East led to the impressive, beautiful cities of the Mongol Empire.

In 1747, the first use of the term *civil engineer* coincided with the founding in France of the first engineering school, the National School of Bridges and Highways. Its graduates researched and formalized theories on many subjects, including fluid pressure. John Smeaton (1724–1792), British designer of the Eddystone Lighthouse, was the first to actually call himself a civil engineer, thus separating his work from that of the military engineer. The eighteenth century also witnessed the founding in Britain of the world's first engineering society, the Institution of Civil Engineers.

Civil engineers of the 1800s designed sanitation and water-supply systems, laid out highways and railroads, and planned cities. Mechanical engineering had its beginnings in England and Scotland and grew out of the inventions of Scottish engineer James Watt and the textile machinists of the Industrial Revolution. The rise of the British machine-tool industry caused interest in the study of mechanical engineering to skyrocket, both in Europe and elsewhere.

In the nineteenth century, the gradual growth of knowledge in the area of electricity eventually led to the most popular branch of the engineering profession today—electrical and electronics engineering. Electronics engineering came into prominence through the work of various English and German scientists and with the development in the United States of the vacuum tube and the transistor in the 1900s. Today electrical and electronics engineers outnumber all other engineers in the world.

Chemical engineering came into existence in the 1800s through the spread of industrial processes involving chemical reactions to produce textiles, food, metals, and a variety of other materials. By 1880, the use of chemicals in manufacturing had created a new industry, mass production of chemicals. The design and operation of this industry's plants became the main function of the new chemical engineer.

The twentieth century brought many other branches of the profession into prominence, and the number of people working in the engineering field increased dramatically. Artificial hearts, airplanes, computers, lasers, plastics, space travel, nuclear energy, and television are only a few of the scientific and technological breakthroughs that engineers helped to bring about from 1900 to 2000.

Breakthroughs in fields like nanotechnology and sensors assure that the field of engineering will continue to grow and expand. The twenty-first century holds many exciting opportunities for engineers to continue the tradition of improving our lives.

MAJOR ENGINEERING AREAS AND SPECIALTIES

Although the U.S. Department of Labor lists twenty-five engineering specialties with at least eighty-five different subdivisions, it is important to keep in mind that there are six areas of engineering that form the core of the profession. These areas are:

- Chemical engineering
- Civil engineering
- Electrical and electronics engineering
- Industrial engineering
- Materials science engineering
- Mechanical engineering

Preparation in any one of these areas will provide a solid foundation for a wide range of engineering specialties.

Undergraduate study in any one of these areas will be adequate preparation for many career options after graduation, including graduate study in the same area or another area of engineering. Study of one of these basic areas of engineering is also excellent preparation for the study of business, law, or medicine. In a time when it is important to keep many options open for future career development, pursuit of one of these disciplines can provide flexibility and satisfaction throughout one's professional life.

Through the years each traditional engineering area has developed increasingly more focused specialties. Today some of those specialties have become engineering professions in their own right. A good example of a specialty becoming an engineering profession is environmental engineering.

There are other engineering areas that can either be pursued as a specialty area within one of the previously discussed engineering areas or pursued as a college major in their own right at institutions that offer a more in-depth preparation for these fields. Some of these fields include:

- Aerospace engineering
- Agricultural engineering
- Automotive engineering
- Biomedical engineering
- Computer engineering
- Environmental engineering
- Manufacturing engineering
- Petroleum engineering

This group of engineering areas allows one to specialize in an industry or a particular application of engineering knowledge. These fields are discussed further in Chapters 13–21.

THE TECHNOLOGY TEAM

It is evident that engineers address the challenges that face the society in which they live. From the Egyptian pyramids and the compounds used for medieval swords to composite tennis rackets, engineers are problem-solvers. They link scientific discovery with day-to-day applications.

Engineers are team players who improve products, processes, and services. Therefore, it is important to understand the technology team on which engineers participate. The engineer is a part of a team of specialists whose goal is to apply scientific knowledge and practical experience to solve problems. This "technology team" consists of scientists, engineers, technicians, and craftsworkers. Everyone on the team works together to solve a problem or to invent a useful device or system. In learning about the makeup and function of the technology team, you can develop an understanding of technology as a whole and of how it is put to use.

At one end of the spectrum of technology is the scientist. The *scientist's* purpose is to discover knowledge. He or she seeks to uncover new facts and to learn more truths about the natural world. Furthermore, scientists seek to explain the facts that they discover by developing new theorems or theories that relate causes and effects in the natural systems they investigate. In their work, scientists seek to know rather than to apply. In other words, their principal concern is not the application of the new knowledge they have discovered but simply the discovery of that knowledge itself. Some scientists are interested in developing applications of science and scientific methods, but the principal activity of even these individuals remains the discovery of new knowledge.

In contrast to the scientist, the *engineer* is interested primarily in the application of scientific knowledge about the natural world and in discovering facts about the artificial world created by humans. The primary responsibility of engineers, as a part of the technology team, is in conceiving and planning efforts to apply scientific knowledge to solve problems. They design and plan developmental projects, production processes, operations and maintenance procedures, and so on. Their activities are devoted to designs and plans to achieve certain results. These results almost always benefit society; however, the purpose beyond that is to achieve this benefit at a minimum cost in money, materials, and time. In an effort to achieve efficient results, the engineers attempt to forecast the behavior of a system they have designed or to predict the accomplishments of a planned program. All the benefits and costs of proposed activities must be predicted by engineers, who are the principal planners of the technology team.

It is the *technician's* responsibility to see that the engineer's design or plan is implemented. While the engineer is concerned mainly with designing or conceiving, the technician is concerned with doing. The technician may be involved in time-and-motion studies or in supervising the construction of a facility designed and planned by the engineer. In accomplishing such work, the engineering technician is more specialized and more concerned with a particular application of scientific knowledge than is the engineer who must plan complex systems. Basically, the technician utilizes science and mathematics to solve technical problems contained within the broad framework of designs and plans conceived by an engineer. Additionally, he or she utilizes instruments and certain tools to measure and monitor the quality and performance of completed systems. However, the technician's principal function is not to utilize tools but to see that designs and plans are implemented by the craftsworkers who do use tools. The technician lies in the occupational spectrum closest to the engineer.

At the opposite end of the technology spectrum from the scientist are the skilled *craftsworkers*, who use their hands and special skills rather than science or scientific knowledge. They are more likely to employ tools than instruments in their work, and they must develop a high degree of skill in using these tools. Craftsworkers include electricians, instrument makers, machinists, and model makers. The craftsworker, too, has an important position on the technology team, and, to some degree, the overall success of the technical system depends on his or her skill in utilizing tools and his or her concern for good workmanship in construction.

WHAT AN ENGINEER DOES

Engineers plan, design, construct, and manage the use of natural and human resources. In addition to human skill, engineering also involves science, mathematics, and aesthetics. As stated, engineers solve problems. They design cars, spacecraft, and medical devices; they can build buildings and bridges; they solve environmental problems; they apply computer technology to a wide range of problems. Because engineers have a strong interest and ability in science, mathematics, and technology, they are team leaders who can take an idea from concept to reality.

There are seven major functions that an engineer can pursue within all branches of engineering. These functions are:

• **Research.** Look for new principles and processes by using scientific and mathematical concepts, experimentation, or inductive reasoning.

• **Development.** Creatively use the results of research and intelligent application of new ideas to invent a working model of a new machine, chemical process, or computer chip.

• **Design.** Choose the methods and materials necessary to meet technical requirements and performance specifications when a new product is being designed.

- **Construction.** Prepare the construction site, arrange the materials, and organize personnel and equipment.
- **Production.** Take care of plant layout, the selection of equipment with regard to the human and economic factors, and the choice of processes and tools as well as checking the flow of materials and components and performing testing and inspections.
- **Operation.** Control manufacturing and processing plants and machines as well as determining procedures and supervising the workforce.
- **Management.** Analyze customer needs, solve economic problems, and deal in a variety of other areas depending on the type of organization involved.

In addition to diversity of function, engineering is performed in a wide variety of settings. Many engineers are found in manufacturing industries, and others work in engineering and architectural firms; public utilities; business and management consulting; federal, state, and local governments; and colleges and universities. In addition, engineers can be found in nonmanufacturing settings such as banks and hospitals.

WHAT ARE SOME ENGINEERING CAREER PATHS?

There are five primary career paths that engineers follow: industry, consulting, government, academic, or Internet.

The Industry Career Path

The first career path is in industry. In another book I wrote about engineering careers, *Great Jobs for Engineering Majors*, I explained that "Industry has always provided engineers with an abundant and diverse range of career paths leading to personal and professional growth." However, the industry career path has undergone dramatic changes in recent years, and the old image of industry is no longer accurate. Most industrial settings are now high-tech workplaces demanding high levels of engineering expertise to solve problems related to researching, developing, and designing new products and manufacturing those products in a cost-efficient manner. Some of the other areas of industry in which engineers tend to work are accounting and finance, administration, information systems processing, marketing and sales, and technical/professional services.

Therefore, there are numerous opportunities for leadership responsibilities in the industrial setting, and these opportunities are coming earlier and earlier in engineers' careers because of the demand for the new knowledge that graduating engineers possess. Since engineers understand product design, manufacture, and distribution, the industrial career path can lead engineers to the executive level in many companies. In addition, it is most likely that engineers in industry will have obtained advanced degrees in engineering and/or business administration during the course of their employment. This means that they not only have knowledge of the engineering side of the industry but also of the business side. As a result, they can become strong candidates for such positions as plant manager, vice president, president, and chief executive officer (CEO).

The Consulting Career Path

The second career path is in consulting. In this career path, engineers work for companies that are hired by other companies to perform engineering tasks, design tasks, or management tasks. What exactly does this mean?

Engineers who work for engineering consulting firms perform engineering tasks for other companies or organizations, and when their job is done, they move on to a new project for another company or organization. For example, if your city or town wanted to build a new highway for the new mall that is being constructed, officials would most likely hire a company that has many civil engineers knowledgeable about how to design and build highways and bridges in a cost-effective manner. That engineering consulting company would come to the city and build the new highway. When the engineers were finished, they would go on to work on another highway project for another neighborhood, city, or state that needed their expertise.

Engineers who work for design consulting firms do the work necessary to design a device for another company that wants to offer a new product to its customers. For example, if a company wanted to make new in-line skates that are lighter and faster, it could hire a design consulting firm that has engineers who would work only on the new skate design until the design met the requirements of the company that hired the engineers.

Once the company could use the design to manufacture new in-line skates in a cost-effective manner, the design consulting firm would begin working on another product for another company.

All consulting engineers work on numerous projects with different types of organizations and people. Some engineers pursue consulting careers early to help them decide where they ultimately want to work, and others pursue consulting later in their careers when they have become real experts in their field—at this point clients are willing to pay them very well for their knowledge.

The Government Career Path

A third career path for engineers is in government. Federal, state, and local governments are excellent employers. The U.S. Department of Defense employs a wide range of engineers in both civilian and enlisted positions for agencies and installations throughout the world. Likewise, NASA employs diverse types of engineers in the space program. While many aerospace engineers have positions with this government agency, NASA also hires almost every type of engineer because of the great variety and creativity of its projects. Similarly, organizations such as the FBI, CIA, and NSA (National Security Agency) hire different types of engineers, particularly those with strong foreign-language abilities.

There are government agencies that tend to hire a larger number of one type of engineer over another. For example, the Food and Drug Administration is a major employer of biomedical and chemical engineers. The U.S. Environmental Protection Agency and the U.S. Army Corps of Engineers employ more civil and environmental engineers and the Federal Aviation Administration hires myriad electrical engineers. In some cases, like the Environmental Protection Agency, engineers find jobs at the state, local, and federal levels.

The Academic Career Path

The fourth career path for engineers is the academic path. This means that many engineers teach. While most engineers who teach have received either a master's degree or Ph.D. and teach in colleges and universities, some engineers decide to obtain state teaching certificates immediately after completing a bachelor's degree. The teaching certificate qualifies them to teach math and/or science in middle schools and high schools in the state where they live.

Engineers who pursue the academic career path enjoy sharing knowledge with others. They may have had experience teaching or tutoring and know that this is satisfying to them. In most cases, engineers who teach in middle schools and high schools, as well as those who teach in colleges and universities, have looked at their personal values, strengths, and interests and determined that teaching is the best career path for them.

The Internet Career Path

Finally, a new career path for engineers has emerged. The Internet career path has opened new possibilities for graduating engineers. The phenomenon of the Internet was developed by engineers and continues to provide many career opportunities for them, whether they are electrical and computer engineers or industrial engineers and computer scientists.

While there are Internet opportunities for engineers with companies that are closely associated with the Internet, like Amazon.com, eBay, or Priceline.com, there are also Internet career possibilities with more traditional companies such as General Electric, General Motors, or Delta Airlines. These companies have realized that to be successful today they need to use the Internet to get their products to their customers more quickly and cost effectively. Increasing numbers of career opportunities will exist for engineers who possess the right set of skills for the Internet career path.

Other Career Paths for Engineers

In addition to these five primary engineering career paths, many engineering graduates decide to pursue graduate and professional degrees. While some obtain advanced degrees in engineering, others decide to pursue graduate and professional degrees in such areas as medicine and law. These advanced degrees offer increased opportunities for career advancement in any career path the individual pursues.

Many factors in today's global economy mean that the future projections for engineering are excellent. This is especially true in areas such as electrical and computer engineering, environmental engineering, materials engineering, manufacturing engineering, civil engineering, and biomedical engineering.

However, engineering opportunities have always had a tendency to go in cycles. Aerospace engineering is a good example, as is chemical engineering. The changing economy and world events impact opportunities for engineering. For example, military actions in the world require innovations in surveillance equipment and defense technologies. Likewise, new discoveries about DNA lead to innovations in pharmaceuticals. This means that new and emerging industries will create competition in a global market. The electronics and health-care industries are examples of growing industries that are providing new opportunities for engineers.

Federal and state governments regularly publish documents that provide current and up-to-date information on the future outlook and projections that apply to a wide range of career fields. The *Occupational Outlook Handbook* (www.bls.gov/oco/) published by the U.S. Department of Labor is a good source of information in this area. But a word to the wise—in deciding which engineering area you wish to pursue, do not rely solely on information about the engineering disciplines that are currently in demand. There are always openings for all types of engineers. It is best to pursue the area that matches your personal strengths and is of most interest to you!

Studying what interests you will most likely be easier, and, therefore, you are more likely to do better in your course work. Good grades in any engineering major will assure that job opportunities and graduate school study are future options. However, the most important reason for pursuing what most interests you is that you will be more likely to be successful and satisfied with your career choice in the years to come.

C H A P T E R

PREPARING FOR A SUCCESSFUL ENGINEERING CAREER

Contributed by David Siegel, National Society for Professional Engineers; Leann Yoder, Executive Director, Junior Engineering Technical Society; and Liz Glazer, ABET, Inc.

There are many reasons for choosing an engineering career. The Junior Engineering Technical Society (JETS) gives ten reasons:

1. Change the world
2. Be creative
3. Work with great people
4. Make a difference
5. Never be bored
6. Make a big salary
7. Solve problems
8. Travel
9. Enjoy job flexibility
10. Love your work *and* live your life, too!

These are important reasons to pursue a career in engineering. However, what does it take to do so and how can you get there? This chapter will help answer those questions.

Engineering is built on math and science, so it is important to take as much math and science as possible. In fact, most engineering schools require four years of high school math and three years of high school science. Therefore, preparation for an engineering career ideally begins early.

Middle and high school math and science courses will begin to open doors for studying engineering in college. However, if you did not take the recommended math and science in middle school and high school, do not give up your dream of becoming an engineer! Consider taking courses in summer school to get caught up. If you are out of high school, look into taking community college courses in math and science. If you think you would love engineering but have a fear of math and/or science, get involved in some of the extracurricular programs that help people understand math and science better. There are lists of organizations that offer such programs at the end of this chapter and throughout the book.

Building a math and science foundation by taking the courses or over-coming your fear or lack of high school math and science are the first steps to a rewarding career in engineering. The field of engineering needs more well-prepared people. Take the time, make the effort, and prepare to join this profession that makes a difference now and in the future.

WHAT SHOULD YOU STUDY BEFORE GOING TO COLLEGE?

As mentioned, it is very important to take as many high school mathematics and science classes as possible. The math courses should be algebra I and II, geometry, trigonometry, and calculus. The science courses should include biology, chemistry, and physics. Chemistry and physics are required courses in undergraduate engineering programs; therefore, take as many high school chemistry and physics courses as possible. If you are able to take honors and advanced placement (AP) courses in math and science that is certainly advisable. They will give you a more solid foundation for succeeding in college courses.

English, social studies, and foreign language courses are all necessary to be admitted into college engineering programs. Computer, economics, history, and public speaking courses are also highly recommended. In addition, it is a good idea to take courses that interest to you. They might just help guide you toward a particular engineering specialty.

To be sure that you meet the basic educational requirements that will be expected when you enter an engineering major in college, it is important to compare the courses you will have taken to those that JETS recommends. Although admissions requirements differ from school to school, you should have the core classes listed below. In addition, you will want to show that you are well rounded by having a wide range of experiences and knowledge. So along with the core courses, it is important to take courses in history/social studies, geography, computers, and the arts. The JETS recommended core classes include:

Language Arts. Four years, including English, speech, and
   communications
Math. Four years, including algebra I and II, geometry, trigonometry,
   and calculus
Science. Four years, including biology, chemistry, and physics
Second Language. Three years

Plus, don't forget to take standardized tests such as the PSAT, SAT, and ACT to demonstrate your preparation and aptitude for studying engineering. Strive to achieve a combined score of at least 1000 on the SAT and 20 on the ACT.

Today most admissions officers at engineering colleges and universities are also looking for well-rounded students. Extracurricular activities during high school are important in reflecting this. Being a member of math- and science-related clubs will demonstrate strong and consistent interests related to engineering. However, participation in athletics, student government, service organizations, and cultural activities are also important. All of these activities demonstrate the ability to work with other people and to lead groups.

In addition to the information in this book, obtain more information about careers in engineering from your school counselors and teachers. Information is also available from local chapters of the National Society of Professional Engineers and professional associations in the specific area of engineering that interests you.

A valuable resource is JETS, which exists to increase interest in and awareness of engineering- and technology-based careers by helping students see the critical role engineers play in the world around us and how engineers make a difference. By providing programs and resources, JETS lets students explore, assess, and experience engineering firsthand. From student competitions to assessment tools and career explorations materials, JETS can help you plan for a rewarding future in engineering. To learn more about JETS, visit their website at jets.org.

HOW TO CHOOSE A COLLEGE

The next step in pursuing an engineering career is selecting a college or university where you will study engineering. College and university websites and catalogs are important tools in comparing and evaluating engineering education programs. Appendix A provides a listing of all U.S. colleges and universities that offer accredited engineering degrees. It is important to learn how to read these institutions' web pages and catalogs so that you will be able to ask good questions and get full information on the requirements for and expectations of each program.

The first step is to look at entrance requirements. Many colleges and universities have minimum entrance requirements. If you are not sure if you meet the entrance requirements, speak to the admissions officer of the college or university. Admissions officers are willing to discuss how they evaluate applications.

The second step is to look at the engineering majors and specialties offered at each college or university. Do the colleges and universities that you are considering offer the type of engineering major that interests you? Will you have to maintain a certain grade point average in order to declare a major in your area of interest? If a certain grade point average is required to declare a major, what percentage of entering students are able to maintain the average required for the major in which you are interested? If you are unsure about your major, does the school provide a broad enough introduction to engineering that you will have sufficient options and time in order to select a major? Does the school provide a support system to help you decide on a major, or are you expected to reach this decision on your own?

While the college website and catalog should include the costs of tuition, fees, and room and board, it is important to remember these will not be your only costs. You also will buy books, pay for travel to and from school, buy personal supplies, pay for entertainment expenses, and incur other day-to-day costs. Therefore, it may be important to look at any financial aid available. Be sure to ask each college or university you are considering for information on all grants, scholarships, loans, Reserve Officers' Training Corps (ROTC), and work-study programs that may help you finance your education. In addition, it is always advisable to meet with the financial aid director to discuss your specific needs.

"College Nights" are an excellent opportunity to gather information on admissions requirements, costs of attendance, and financial aid opportunities. Start going to these events throughout your time at high school. Don't wait until your junior year. Get to know the admissions people. However, nothing substitutes for a visit to the college campus. It is important to see and feel the campus environment as well as the engineering environment. Visits are the best way to determine if there will be a good fit between you and the college you choose to attend.

HOW TO MANAGE YOUR ENGINEERING CAREER WHILE IN COLLEGE

Your career in engineering will not start when you leave college. It will actually start while you are an undergraduate student. When you pick a major (mechanical engineering, chemical engineering, biomedical engineering, etc.) you have taken the first step in your career. It is *not* an irreversible step, but it is a step!

Bachelor's degree programs in engineering take four or five years to complete. In general, the first two years concentrate on mathematics and the physical sciences, with introductory engineering courses and courses in English and the social sciences. The last two years include required courses in engineering and particularly required courses in the major. In addition, engineering students take technical electives and "free" electives. Technical electives are usually engineering courses from disciplines outside of your major. Free electives are either any course outside of engineering that the student wishes to take or any course on a list of electives approved by the engineering department.

There are also transfer programs called "two-plus-two" or "two-plus-three" programs. These programs combine two years of study at a community college and then two or three more years of study after transferring to a participating four-year college. In some cases, both bachelor's and master's degrees are awarded at the end of a "two-plus-three" program.

There are also five- or six-year cooperative engineering education programs (co-op). In these programs, engineering students alternate periods of academic study with periods of paid engineering-related work in industry. By graduation, students in co-op programs usually have more than one year of progressively responsible engineering experience. This makes them very competitive in the job market.

Most, but not all, bachelor's degree programs in engineering are accredited by ABET, Inc. To become an ABET-accredited engineering or engineering technology program, each engineering department must demonstrate that its program has published educational objectives and that it is continually assessing and evaluating how those objectives are being achieved by its graduates. These objectives are often published on engineering department websites and provide potential students with valuable information on program emphasis. In addition, ABET requires that engineering students be able to demonstrate a specific set of minimum outcomes at the time of graduation. For example, students should have the ability to:

- Apply knowledge of mathematics, science, and engineering
- Design and conduct experiments as well as analyze and interpret data
- Design a system, component, or process to meet desired needs within realistic constraints, including economic, environmental, social, political, ethical, health, safety, manufacturability, and sustainability
- Function on multidisciplinary teams
- Identify, formulate, and solve engineering problems
- Understand and take professional and ethical responsibility
- Communicate effectively
- Comprehend the impact of engineering solutions in a global, economic, environmental, and societal context
- Recognize the need for lifelong learning
- Engage in activities that further learning
- Stay attuned to contemporary issues
- Use the techniques, skills, and modern engineering tools necessary for engineering practice

In order for an academic program to achieve these student outcomes, the faculty must look not only at curriculum but at the total experience that students have, including the skill sets they bring from high school as well as the co-op and extracurricular experience they have in college. When looking at engineering schools and specific engineering programs, it is important to consider the educational objectives that they have set for their programs and the resources they provide to help students achieve the required outcomes. Careful examination of the school's and the program's websites is very important.

To locate accredited engineering programs, begin by going to ABET's website, abet.org. In addition to looking at college and university websites, it is recommended that students become familiar with the criteria that selected professional associations have set for their chosen discipline. ABET is made up of member societies that can help you not only understand careers in their specific field of engineering, but also their recommended criteria for engineering education in that field. In addition, many of these societies offer scholarships to deserving individuals. See Appendix C for scholarship information and Appendix D for ABET member societies.

The engineering experience that you gain during your college career should extend beyond your classes and labs. Internships and summer jobs in an engineering setting can be important to your career. However, many engineering employers place more value on co-op experience.

Co-op is an engineering educational approach that began at the University of Cincinnati in 1906 when Professor Herman Schneider's research indicated that it was too costly for engineering employers to train new engineers after graduation. For nearly one hundred years, hundreds of thousands of engineers have alternated periods of paid work experience related to their major with periods of academic course work. These co-op graduates completed their undergraduate education with a four-year degree and more than one year of engineering experience with increasing responsibilities. Many collegiate engineering schools still offer co-op programs today because they are so highly valued by industry. Generally these are five-year programs, and numerous studies have indicated that the fifth year is well worth the investment. Year after year, surveys have shown that the starting salaries of co-op engineering graduates have been significantly higher than those of non co-op graduates. However, most co-op graduates will say that the real benefit of the program is the experience they gained and the increased awareness of what they enjoy and want to do as professional engineers.

While there are many outstanding co-op engineering programs, those at the University of Cincinnati, the University of Detroit, Drexel University,

Purdue University, Georgia Institute of Technology, Northeastern University, and Virginia Tech are among the oldest and most well-established.

BEYOND THE UNDERGRADUATE DEGREE—WORK OR GRADUATE SCHOOL?

When the bachelor's degree in engineering is awarded, you will have many career options. You can choose to pursue your engineering career in a wide variety of areas such as industry, business, consulting, marketing, management, government, research, university teaching, sales, and the military.

In addition to these options, many engineers eventually pursue study beyond the bachelor's degree. Some go on to medical school or law school. Others obtain graduate degrees in business or management. Many pursue master's and doctoral degrees in engineering disciplines.

PROFESSIONAL LICENSING

After graduation from college, you can become a registered or licensed engineer in the state or states in which you work. Engineers who become registered or licensed are known as "professional engineers." They are able to put the designation P.E. after their names. This designation conveys a level of commitment to the engineering profession that is highly valued in a number of industries and engineering disciplines.

According to the National Council of Examiners for Engineering and Surveying (NCEES), there is a growing demand for engineers who have become licensed engineers. In part, this demand is due to the perception that P.E.s are committed to the highest ethical and professional standards and to the practice of engineering.

Many employers want P.E.s on their team because that designation provides credibility to clients and to customers. In very competitive fields within engineering, this can be an important advantage. For civil engineers and for engineers with consulting engineering firms, the P.E. designation is not just an advantage, it is often a requirement. In some industries the designation is highly recommended for management positions. Consequently, becoming a licensed engineer could be one of the most important career decisions you will make.

The National Council of Examiners for Engineering and Surveying identifies the following benefits of becoming a P.E.

• **Promotability.** Many employers require licensure for advancement to senior engineering positions. This is particularly true when companies are engaged in internal and external partnership agreements.

• **High Salaries.** Licensed P.E.s earn higher salaries than nonlicensed engineers.

• **The P.E. Title.** Professional engineers can sign and seal documents submitted to a client or a public authority and legally represent themselves to the public as "professional engineers."

• **Career Advantages.** Only P.E.s are eligible to work legally as engineering consultants.

Licensing Requirements

It takes several years to become a P.E. The length of time varies from state to state as well as individual to individual. However, most registered or licensed engineers go through three phases to achieve this designation.

• **Stage 1.** Graduation from an ABET-EAC engineering program. (EAC is the Engineering Accreditation Commission.)

• **Stage 2.** Passage of the Fundamentals of Engineering (FE) exam. This was formerly called the Engineer-In-Training (EIT) exam. If you see references to the EIT exam, it is the same thing as the FE exam. This is an engineering and science fundamentals test.

• **Stage 3.** Passage of the Principles and Practice of Engineering (PE) exam. This is a test of knowledge in a specific branch of engineering (i.e., civil engineering, electrical engineering, etc.). The PE exam tests the engineer's ability to apply engineering principles and judgment to professional problems.

Tips for Meeting the Licensing Requirements

If you think that you will eventually want, or need, to become a licensed engineer, you should plan to attend a college or university with programs approved by the Engineering Accreditation Commission (EAC) of ABET. You need to be careful when selecting your program of study. Some programs within a college or university are accredited by ABET, while others are not. Lists of ABET-EAC programs are available at abet.org.

The next step in the licensing process is passing the Fundamentals of Engineering (FE) exam, formerly the EIT exam. It is administered every fall and spring by state engineering registration boards.

The chair of the Engineering Deans' Council of the American Society for Engineering Education recently stated that engineering students benefited in the long run if they took the FE exam before graduation. This is sound advice when you consider how much knowledge you accumulate as an undergraduate. Two or three years after graduation, it can be extremely difficult to recall concepts and facts necessary to pass the FE exam.

All state boards of licensure administer the same FE examination. The exam is produced by the NCEES. However, the dates that the exams are administered can vary slightly from state to state. It is necessary to apply to take the exam well in advance.

Engineering students are advised to take the exam during their senior year in college. Therefore, it is recommended that the semester or quarter prior to starting your senior year in college you contact the engineering licensure board in the state or states where you plan to become licensed (see the NCEES website at ncees.org for a list of state engineering licensure boards). They will be able to tell you when and where the FE exam will be administered during your senior year and the application deadline.

The FE exam consists of two four-hour periods. The morning exam tests comprehension and knowledge as well as evaluation, analysis, and application. The afternoon exam is composed of problem sets from seven subject areas: statics, dynamics, and mechanics of materials; fluid mechanics; electrical theory; and economic analysis.

The FE exam is an open-book test. However, states do vary in the amount of material that you are allowed to bring into the exam. This is important information to ask about when you contact the state board of licensure regarding test dates and deadlines.

The third step in becoming a licensed engineer is fulfilling your state's requirements for years of professional experience. The minimum number of years of professional engineering experience is two. While this requirement varies from state to state, most states require four years of acceptable progressive experience.

It is important for you to know that in some cases your participation in a university-sponsored co-op program may count toward this experience. The semesters or quarters that you co-op (work) will be documented on your academic transcript for review by the licensure board.

Finally, you will need to pass the PE exam. This exam will test your in-depth knowledge of a specific field of engineering. If you are a mechanical engineer, the exam you take will test your ability to apply mechanical engineering principles to real-life problems. Likewise, if you are a chemical engineer, you will be tested on the engineering principles in that discipline.

ADDITIONAL SOURCES OF INFORMATION

Further information on preparing for a career in engineering is available from the following organizations:

ABET, Inc.
111 Market Place, Suite 1050
Baltimore, MD 21202
abet.org

Junior Engineering Technical Society (JETS)
1420 King St., Suite 405
Alexandria, VA 22314
jets.org

National Council of Examiners for Engineering and Surveying (NCEES)
P.O. Box 1686
Clemson, SC 29633
ncees.org

National Society of Professional Engineers (NSPE)
1420 King St.
Alexandria, VA 22314
nspe.org

CHAPTER 3

BUILDING A SOLID FOUNDATION FOR YOUR ENGINEERING CAREER

Contributed by Junior Engineering Technical Society (JETS)

PREPARE FOR ENGINEERING MATHEMATICS

While most engineers don't sit around doing math problems all day, there's a lot of math in the college engineering curriculum. Here's some advice gleaned from college counselors and professors to help you get off to a good start. "Calculus is the easy part of the calculus," says one math professor. He says most of his students get tripped up on the algebra behind the calculations. Getting the algebra down solid helps you get off to a good start.

How solid is solid? Here's what some experts say: It's hard to get a better grade in your next math class than you did on the previous one because most math is cumulative. Just passing a class with a C or D typically doesn't give you enough knowledge to be successfully in the next level. One math professor even went as far as to say that students should consider 700 on the math portion of the SAT as the hurdle to feel prepared. Don't panic if you scored less or have had some Bs or Cs in math. Just take the time to go back and do some additional work to strengthen areas of weakness before moving on to more advanced classes in a college engineering program.

Consider fortifying any shaky areas of algebra and other precalculus topics with tutoring, math club, self-study, or a class at a local community college before heading off to your first year in a college engineering program. It is a small price to pay for getting off to a good start. In addition, bookstores have a number of great self-help math books, including *Algebra for Dummies* and others in that series. There also are many excellent online math resources. Use your favorite search engine to get the help you need on particular topics.

Even if you've had calculus in high school, consider starting with calculus I in college—or maybe backtracking to precalculus. These classes are typically taught in much greater depth in college, sometimes with different emphasis. Some colleges require their students to take calculus without a graphing computer to ensure they know the math. This can be a challenge if you and your graphing calculator were joined at the hip in high school.

ENGINEERING APTITUDES

All people have aptitudes. They are natural talents, special abilities, and the capability of learning to do certain things. As a group, engineers tend to have strong aptitudes in spatial visualization, analytical reasoning, memory for design, and mathematical ability.

Spatial Visualization

Many engineering classes require you to look at technical drawings or visualize object in three dimensions. Students with lower aptitude and skill levels in this area are at a distinct disadvantage. To test your spatial skill, try putting together a 3-D puzzle. Another good test it to fold a piece of paper randomly several times and then punch a hole through all layers using a paper punch. Imagine where the holes will be when you open it up. You might want to draw out where you think the dots will be on a separate sheet of paper. Open up your folded sheet and compare the actual results with what you imagined.

If spatial visualization isn't your strength, don't despair. There are many games and activities that can help build your skill level and make those engineering classes easier for you. One game recommended by several engineering professors is Tetris. So go have some fun building your spatial skills.

Analytical Reasoning

Individuals who are able to organize concepts, arrange ideas in a logical sequence, and classify things are considered to have analytical reasoning. This aptitude helps you to organize information to solve word problems, set up science experiments, and plan work.

This aptitude is generally tested by looking at four pictures or words and identifying which of the group does not belong in the set. If you're good at organizing information and word problems, chances are you are strong in this aptitude. People with high inductive reasoning can take unrelated pieces of information and detect common threads that join them into a pattern. This makes them good at diagnosing problems and solving them—an important skill for engineers.

Memory for Design

Whether looking at architectural plans or schematics for a circuit board, memory for design can be helpful. Memory for design is tested by looking for twelve seconds at a collection of straight lines running at different angles—some running parallel and some connecting. The design is abstract, resembling no identifiable shape. On a sheet of paper, subjects then try to connect the dots to form the same design from memory. This aptitude is valuable in designing structures and other facilities as well as products such as engines, machinery, and equipment.

Mathematical Ability

While mathematical ability is a key foundation for engineering, some students who score low in math because of difficulties with the computational portion may still be good engineers thanks to computers. What is critical is the ability to understand and apply core mathematical concepts to engineering problems. Understanding the concepts behind the math and being able to set up problems are actually more critical than the ability to do the "number crunching." This ability depends more on spatial visualization and analytical reasoning than computational skills. Students who don't score high in math may still find engineering a good fit; they will just have to work harder in the area of academic study. Conversely, students who have good grades in math but don't have strong aptitudes in structural visualization and analytical reasoning may be better suited to applying their math skills in a field such as accounting, financial analysis, economics, marketing research, or social or physical sciences.

For insight into your current level of readiness for the math and other analytical components of an engineering program, consider taking JETS Assess from JETS. This self-administered academic survey helps assess academic readiness to study engineering and identifies areas of strength and areas for further study and development. For more information, visit www .jets.org/programs/assess.

BEYOND MATH AND SCIENCE

Engineering isn't just about math and science. Curiosity, excellent communications skills, experience with teamwork and leadership, travel experiences, and knowledge of arts and literature along with interests and hobbies help provide the necessary background from which to draw the insight and creativity needed to solve engineering challenges. To help people and develop creative solutions, engineers need to be well-rounded people, with lots of experiences to draw on.

In addition, having other experiences and interests to draw on—music, sports, dance, drama, art, theater, or student government—can provide balance and a nice break from intensive engineering classes.

ENGINEERING TECHNOLOGY—AN ALTERNATE CHOICE

If you know a four-year engineering program isn't for you but still want to work in engineering, engineering technology is a great choice. Engineering technicians are the applications people on a team who work with engineers in the design process and often are heavily involved in implementation or ongoing maintenance of a project. Two-year (associate's) and four-year (bachelor's) degrees are offered in engineering technology. Two-year degrees in a wide range of engineering specialties are offered at technical institutes and schools, community colleges, and extension programs of universities. Four-year degrees in engineering technology are offered by more than 200 schools and universities. Visit ABET, Inc.'s website, abet.org, to find one.

There are many ways to continue to explore engineering careers and engineering aptitudes. JETS (jets.org) provides a number of resources that can be helpful to you, including the following:

• *Pre-Engineering Times.* An e-newsletter that focuses on different engineering fields and provides activities that can help one learn and develop the aptitudes discussed in this chapter

• **Explore Online.** Videos and information about engineers and what they do

• **ASSESS.** A toolkit for high school students to gauge academic preparedness for engineering

• **TEAMS.** A national academic competition to apply math and science to real-world engineering problems

• **JETS Challenge.** A weekly word problem on the JETS website that helps one organize information and solve science and math problems

• **National Engineering Design Challenge (NEDC).** A competition for students to explore, research, design, and build a prototype to empower people with disabilities to succeed in the workplace

• **JETS NEAS+.** A self-administered evaluation of your current level of preparation in engineering basic skills subjects—applied mathematics, science, and reasoning

RESOURCES FOR BUILDING SKILLS

Engineering K–12 Resource Center
engineeringk12.org/precollege

FIRST: For Inspiration and Recognition of Science and Technology
usfirst.org

Future City Competition
futurecity.org

Junior Engineering Technical Society (JETS)
jets.org

MATHCOUNTS
mathcounts.org

NASA for Kids
nasa.gov/audience/forstudents/k-4/index.html

NASA SCIence Files
whyfiles.larc.nasa.gov/kids/inside_treehouse.html

TOYchallenge
sallyridescience.com/toychallenge

TryScience
tryscience.org/home.html

Zoom into Engineering
pbskids.org/zoom/grownups/engineering

CHAPTER

4

FINANCING YOUR ENGINEERING EDUCATION

Newspaper headlines are constantly reporting the rise in college tuition. In fact, the rising cost of going to college continues to exceed national cost of living increases. However, higher education is the ticket to a better life and a more secure future, so cost alone should not deter you from obtaining an engineering education. This is particularly true for people pursuing engineering degrees because there many sources of financial assistance for engineering majors.

While you and your family are expected to meet some of the costs of higher education, there is financial aid to help you make the dream of an engineering degree a reality. In almost every college or school of engineering, there is an associate or assistant dean of engineering who is responsible for undergraduate engineering students issues. These individuals often have knowledge of or leads about options for helping to pay for your education. You and your family should discuss opportunities for applying for scholarships as well as co-op and financial assistance programs designated for engineering students.

In addition, the college or university of your choice will have a financial aid representative on staff whose sole responsibility is to help students apply for all of the available aid programs for which they qualify. These representatives can assist in filling out the various forms and will answer your questions concerning the types and amounts of assistance available.

It is very important to understand the differences among the five types of aid available. Aid can take the form of:

- Scholarships
- Grants
- Loans
- Work-study jobs
- Co-op

SCHOLARSHIPS

A scholarship is a monetary grant to a student who qualifies under a variety of circumstances. There are scholarships for the academically gifted. Others are based on special abilities such as musical talent, athletics, speech, and drama. Occasionally, scholarships may have one or more conditions that must be met in terms of academic ability and/or financial need.

The key point to remember is that a scholarship is a grant, or gift, of money for a specific purpose (education) with specific requirements (talent, academic merit, and/or financial need). It does *not* require repayment. Each institution has its own requirements and qualifications for scholarships. In addition, community organizations, businesses, and professional associations award scholarships to engineering students. A list of engineering associations that offer scholarships is included in Appendix C.

GRANTS

A grant is a gift of financial aid for a specific purpose (education). Similar to a scholarship, it may impose conditions on the recipient and does not require repayment. Sources of grants include the institution itself; local, state, and federal governments; private industry; and groups. Each grant has specific conditions and requirements that must be met. To identify grants for which you might qualify, first, talk to a representative in the financial aid offices of the colleges and universities where you are interested in studying engineering. These professionals will be able to provide information on federal, state and, in some cases, institutional grant programs and the qualifications you need to meet.

Second, at the end of each chapter of this book that covers an engineering discipline, you will find a list of professional associations. Search these websites for grants or scholarships that the associations might offer. If you are a woman or minority, you should also search websites at the end of Chapters 5 and 6.

LOANS

A loan is not a grant or a scholarship. It is a legal obligation that must be repaid. A student loan can be obtained from the learning institution, a bank or savings and loan, or a government agency. The government agency's role is usually limited to insuring the lender—the school, a bank, or a savings and loan—that you will repay the loan according to the terms of the contract.

Certain loans, especially those earmarked for students in high-demand, low-supply career fields, often have special clauses permitting portions of the loan to be cancelled if conditions are met. An example is a loan made to an engineering student who co-ops with a federal agency. According to one such agreement, the loan is cancelled so long as the student works full-time for the agency until the time worked equals the amount of time for which the student received the loan. If the student does not work full-time for the agency, the loan must be repaid with interest.

Keep in mind that all loans must be repaid in some manner. Interest charges are almost always added to an educational loan. Repayment usually does not begin until after you have graduated. There are exceptions to this, so ask lots of questions when applying for educational loans.

It is important to remember that if you do not repay the loan, the lender may take legal action against you to ensure that the loan is repaid. If the federal government guarantees your loan and you fail to pay, then legally your income tax refund checks and your wages can be garnished until the debt is satisfied.

APPLYING FOR FINANCIAL AID

Schools use a confidential statement of income and assets from parents and the student to determine what financial aid a student is eligible for. If the student is independent and does not live at home with his or her parents, then the application will reflect information about the student alone. If you fall under this category, you might want to discuss the options available to you with the financial aid representative before proceeding any further.

Application forms and the confidential statement of assets and income can vary from one school to another. You should determine exactly which forms the school of your choice requires and be certain to submit only those forms. These forms have deadlines for submission, so be sure you have the forms and collect the information in plenty of time to meet this deadline.

Questions on the application will assess the financial condition of the family. From your responses, the financial aid committee can determine an estimate of how much money your family can reasonably be expected to contribute toward your education and how much outside assistance you will require.

This assessment will take into account your family's size, income, assets and liabilities, and the number of family members attending postsecondary educational facilities. Your parents' ages and the resources available to you will also enter into the final analysis.

A standard formula is used to ensure that all students are considered in an impartial manner. Your financial aid administrator should be made aware of any special family circumstances that should be considered in this formula along with the information solicited on the application. This special information should be detailed in a letter, which should be sent with any supporting documentation to the aid representative.

HOW MUCH WILL MY EDUCATION COST?

What a college degree costs depends on the type of institution you select. Private Ivy League universities usually cost a great deal more than state-supported colleges. Each school will, on request, provide you with a breakdown of its student expenses. This is called the "budget." It consists of the following items.

• **Tuition and fees.** This represents the amount you will be charged for your classes.

• **Books and supplies.** This cost will vary based on the type of academic program you have selected. Be sure to ask about special books or equipment (lab supplies and computers) required of students in your program.

• **Housing.** This amount will reflect either rates for available housing on campus (dorms) or, if no housing is available, the prevailing rents in the local community.

• **Meals.** If there is a school cafeteria, the amount will be somewhat fixed. If you must eat out, the cost can vary substantially. Sometimes a set board fee will also include laundry and telephone and computer hookups. Be sure to ask.

• **Personal expenses.** This is your allowance, money for entertainment, personal items, and miscellaneous charges you might incur.

• **Transportation.** This is an allowance for trips from school back to your home, for example.

While these costs can vary, especially if you elect to live at home and attend a local college, these factors must be considered to determine what your college education will really cost. Fill out the following chart to help you determine the basic costs.

Estimating the Cost of Your Education

Tuition and fees	_____
Books and supplies	_____
Room/housing	_____
Board/meals	_____
Personal expenses	_____
Transportation	_____
Other expenses	_____
Total estimated college cost	_____
Estimated family contribution	_____
Estimated aid requirement (subtract estimated family contribution from total estimated college cost)	_____
Total	_____

HOW WILL I KNOW WHAT AID I'LL RECEIVE?

The financial aid office at your school will notify you of its decision in what is called an award letter or award notification form. This will tell you what kind or kinds of aid you can expect and the amounts for which you are eligible. This letter will cover all of the available forms of aid you have qualified for, including scholarships, grants, student employment, and loans. Many institutions call this award a financial aid package.

After you have received this letter, you should notify the financial aid representative that you either accept or decline the aid. Some schools will withdraw the offer of assistance if you do not notify them by a specified deadline.

WORK-STUDY JOBS AND CO-OP

Although these two forms of assistance do not fall under the traditional categories, they may be available to you even if you do not qualify for any other assistance. Work-study assigns you to a specific job, usually on campus, and pays you for every hour you work. This money can be used to supplement scholarships and grants as long as you ensure that your work schedule does not conflict with your education.

A co-op position can add a year to your college life, but it can be of substantial benefit and actually put you ahead of students who were able to attend school full-time. You are assigned to a real-world employer where you will work in an area closely related to your chosen profession. You work certain periods of time and attend school during other periods of time. In doing so, you will gain valuable experience in your field that can make a financial difference when you graduate and pursue your first job. In addition, it may be possible for you to graduate less in debt because engineering salaries, including co-op salaries, tend to be higher than average.

Remember, there is no reason not to get an engineering education. Financial aid programs and scholarships can help you afford the cost of a higher education.

Online Resources for Financial Aid
FastWeb: fastweb.com
FinAid: finaid.org
SAGE Scholars: student-aid.com
Scholarships.com: scholarship.com

CHAPTER

5

WOMEN IN ENGINEERING

Contributed by Melissa Tata, Services Delivery Operations Senior Manager, Dell, Inc.

Women have made major contributions to the field of engineering for many years. Lillian Moller Gilbreth was elected into the National Academy of Engineers and is known for teaching industrial engineering and "being the first person to integrate psychology into concepts of industrial management" (www.engineergirl.org/?id=3145). She is known as the "First Lady of Engineering" and was the first honorary member of the Society of Women Engineers. Another early contributor was Emily Roebling, who supervised the construction of the Brooklyn Bridge as Chief Engineer when her husband became ill in 1872. In 1916, Margaret Ingels, P.E., was the first female to graduate from the University of Kentucky's school of engineering and the first female in the United States to receive a mechanical engineering degree. She went to work for Carrier Engineering Corporation, a pioneer in air-conditioning technology. As a result of her design work and the many articles she wrote and speeches she gave, Ingels has been credited with helping to created widespread acceptance of residential air conditioning.

In 1959, Nathelyne Archie Kennedy, P.E., became the first African-American woman to receive an engineering degree from Prairie View A&M University and the first African-American woman to become a licensed engineer in Texas. An accomplished bridge designer, Kennedy continues to break barriers for women and minorities. She is currently president and CEO of her own company, Nathelyne A. Kennedy & Associates.

These pioneers, and others like them, have paved the way for future generations of women to enter into and succeed in the field of engineering. Obviously, engineering is a great profession for women and men alike as it requires creativity and problem solving skills that are gender neutral, creates improvements to society, and provides recognition for these skills and impacts.

People who succeed in engineering have a solid foundation in math and science, plus a strong aptitude for solving problems and the ability to think logically and breakdown complex problems into manageable parts in order to address them. Both men and women possess these abilities, and the engineering profession needs more talented people. In fact, because of the diverse needs of the population, it is very important that the engineering profession be represented by many different types of people who may have unique creative ideas. For example, a female engineer recognized the need to reassess vehicle air bags that could be unsafe for individuals under five feet tall (typically women and children).

REASONS WOMEN BECOME ENGINEERS

Young women and men share the same reasons for studying engineering. They seek a stable income, status, fun, and the ability to have a positive impact on the community. Engineers have significantly higher starting salaries than do college graduates with bachelor's degrees in many other fields, based on supply and demand, economic principles, and the values of our society.

Engineers frequently work on cross-functional project teams that test and/or develop new technology. They are respected due to the rigor of their education; the challenge of their assignments; and the impact of their products/services. In addition, today, as baby boomers retire, there are more engineering jobs than candidates, especially since enrollment in engineering has declined the last several years. As technology thrives globally, engineers are needed in all parts of the world. In particular, more women engineers are needed to offer their diversity of thought.

The National Academy of Engineering hosts the Engineer Girl (www.engineergirl.org) and Engineer Your Life (www.engineeryourlife.org) websites. These sites provide reasons why girls should consider a career in engineering, such as the fact that engineers tackle the challenges that are important to society.

STATISTICS ON WOMEN IN ENGINEERING

Currently, women represent approximately 20 percent of all engineering graduates. From the late 1960s until the early 1980s, the number of women receiving degrees in science and engineering steadily increased. However, according to the National Science Foundation (www.nsf.gov), which keeps statistics on enrollment in science and engineering, the number of women receiving degrees in science and engineering began to plateau in the mid to late 1980s.

The National Science Foundation reports that women made up 12 percent of the people in science and engineering occupations in 1980. By 2000, women comprised 25 percent of the people in these occupations. However, the growth in representation occurred primarily between 1980 and 1990. Between 1990 and 2000, there was only a 3 percent increase in their participation.

In the field of computing and information sciences, women also continue to lag far behind men in participation. In 2006, 59 percent of all undergraduate degree recipients were women; however, only 21 percent of computing and information sciences graduates were women compared to 37 percent in 1985. In that same year, the National Center for Women and Information Technology (ncwit.org) reported that 51 percent of professional occupations were held by women but only 26 percent of the information technology–related occupations were held by women.

The Society for Women Engineers (SWE) has tried to tailor its message about engineering to girls at an early age. Research from the Extraordinary Women Engineers Project indicates that girls want to be involved in meaningful work that makes a difference (http://www.engineeringwomen.org/pdf/EWEPFinal.pdf).

In a time of critical shortage of engineers in the United States, the decline in women pursuing degrees and careers in engineering and science is a real concern. To maintain our competitive edge, the United States needs more men *and* women coming into the field of engineering.

It is very important to have women represented in the engineering profession because engineering applications affect women, men, and children and creative solutions are needed to address these sometimes unique gender needs. In the book *Science and Engineering Programs: On Target for Women?* Linda Wilson states that "we cannot succeed on many critically important policy matters without the full participation of women and minorities, in both the development and the support of effective policy and action." As a country, we need women to participate in and contribute to research and product design because of their unique needs and perspectives.

Women have consistently shown success in engineering. Studies have shown that the high school years are critical in preparing for an engineering career. However, a study at the University of Michigan found that, in high school, women take fewer math and science courses than men. This phenomenon was not found to be related to lack of ability on the part of high school women but, in many cases, due to lack of adequate information about the need for these courses in most college majors—particularly engineering. This finding points to the importance of high school women knowing what the requirements are for entering college engineering programs.

However, high school preparation in math and science does not fully account for the different rates of participation of women and men in engineering. Factors such as self-confidence; stereotypes about women in engineering; encouragement from family, teachers, counselors, and friends; and opportunities for hands-on experiences related to science and engineering also play key roles in whether a young woman decides to pursue an engineering career. So while women have the same aptitude as men in science and math and often have better grades in high school, they can lack confidence in their capabilities or can place less emphasis on the importance of these subjects, which results in them not performing as well on aptitude tests. Therefore, high school women need to recognize their own skills in the areas of math and science and continue to take these classes throughout high school.

Other research has shown that women often are more interested in the impact that engineering has on the betterment of society than on the technical principles. In recent years, there have been efforts to demonstrate engineering impact in this framework. One result is an increase in the percentage of women in environmental and biomedical engineering.

Because you are reading this book, we think you might want even more information about engineering or more support as you take the math and science courses that will keep your options open when you apply to college. There are many programs available to women interested in engineering. The following sites offer a few suggestions from the Society of Women Engineers (SWE).

Archive of Women in Science and Engineering
http://www.lib.iastate.edu/spcl/wise/wise.html

ASEE Engineering K-12 Center's list of competitions appropriate for high
   school students
http://www.engineeringk12.org/students/How_Do_I_Become_An_
   Engineer/Getting_Involved/default.php

Discover Engineering
http://www.discoverengineering.org/

Engineer Girl
http://www.engineergirl.org/

Expanding Your Horizons
http://www.expandingyourhorizons.org

First—For Inspiration and Recognition of Science and Technology
http://www.usfirst.org/

GEM SET, Girls E-Mentoring Program
http://www.uic.edu/orgs/gem-set/

Girls Scouts USA
http://www.girlscouts.org

Junior Engineering Technical Society (JETS)
http://www.jets.org/

National Engineers Week
http://www.eweek.org

A Sightseer's Guide to Engineering
http://www.engineeringsights.org/

Society of Women Engineers Archives
http://www.reuther.wayne.edu/SWEpath.html

Society of Women Engineers Homepage
http://www.swe.org

Society of Women Engineers Programs & Events
Review the "Girl's" section: http://aspire.swe.org/

Society of Women Engineers Scholarships
http://societyofwomenengineers.swe.org/index.
    php?option=com_content&task=view&id=222&Itemid=111

Women in Science, Technology, Engineering, and
    Mathematics ON THE AIR!
http://www.womeninscience.org/

Books

Baine, C. *Is There An Engineer Inside You?: A Comprehensive Guide To Career Decisions In Engineering*. Calhoun, LA: Bonamy Publishing, 2004.

Pasternak, C. and L. Thornburg. *Cool Careers for Girls Book Series*. Manassas Park, VA: Impact Publications.

ADVICE TO WOMEN ENTERING ENGINEERING

A bachelor's degree in engineering will provide the basic preparation for many exciting opportunities in engineering. You should consider which type of engineering best fits your individual interest.

ASEE Engineering What Is Engineering?
http://www.engineeringk12.org/students/What_Is_Engineering/
　　Engineering_alphabet/default.php

Wikipedia Fields of Engineering
http://en.wikipedia.org/wiki/List_of_engineering_fields

In addition to the technical skill set that you will develop through your education, there are other skills that will greatly facilitate your success in the field of engineering. These skills fall into four categories: writing, public speaking, teamwork, and getting the job done.

The first of these career skills is writing. You will need to communicate your work and your proposals. Reports, memos, letters, and proposals will be read and evaluated by audiences such as management, clients, peers, and so on.

Learning to write so that your ideas are clear and concise will be extremely important. Annual reports, expert testimony, responses to unhappy customers, and replies to regulatory agencies are some of the types of writing that will demand versatile writing skills.

The second skill is public speaking. It is often said that public speaking is not an optional skill for engineers. Presentations are a standard part of the engineering workplace. Sometimes these speeches are impromptu. Speaking is important because various groups will need to be sold on the business and technical merit of your projects. Engineers also need to be able to move past the technical jargon to clearly explain their projects to the public.

It is important to join groups and/or take public speaking courses to improve your speaking ability. Joining a local Toastmasters group (www.Toastmasters.org) is an excellent way to improve public speaking.

The third area is teamwork. Too often engineers take an "engineering only" outlook. It is easy for engineers to see only the technical aspects of their work. However, it is important for engineers to look at the broader issues that are facing their companies or organizations. American industry is increasingly taking a team approach to solving problems. The teams usually are made up of people from diverse disciplines within the organization. The teams may consist of a marketing person, an accountant, legal counsel, and an engineer. There can also be teams of many types of engineers. These cross-functional teams work together to solve a problem or develop a new product.

Finally, it is important to get the job done. Women engineers who are entering the workforce for the first time need to understand that the work environment and the classroom environment differ greatly. Work assignments can overlap and instructions are not always clear and definitive. Priority setting becomes very important. You will also need the ability to create business cases for your projects by assessing the costs and expected benefit.

It is very important to maintain your engineering technical skills and to network with others to continue to learn more about engineering and professional options. One great way to keep up is to join a professional engineering organization for your type of engineering such as the Institute of Electrical and Electronics Engineers (IEEE), the American Society of Mechanical Engineers (ASME), the American Institute of Chemical Engineers (AIChE), or the National Society of Professional Engineers (NSPE) for licensed engineers. There are also terrific organizations like the Society of Women Engineers (SWE), the Society of Hispanic Professional Engineers (SHPE), the National Society of Black Engineers (NSBE), and the American Indian Science and Engineering Society (AISES) to help you generate a strong, diverse engineering network where you can meet mentors to help you develop your field's skills. You can also take on leadership roles in these organizations to practice using those skills. An added advantage of these engineering networks is the interaction you will have with other people who are sometimes scarce in engineering work places, such as women.

Knowing what it takes to successfully get your job done is something that is not consistently taught in the classroom. Incorporating hands-on experience, such as cooperative engineering education (co-op), in your college career can ease the transition from school to work because you will learn to work in an environment that provides support and encouragement. You will learn to ask for help, meet deadlines, and perform as a professional engineer in industry before you graduate from college. This learning is invaluable to the new engineer.

In addition to developing skills beyond their technical expertise, women in engineering need to be prepared to learn from one another. This can be accomplished through networking and mentoring programs. Whether formal or informal, these programs help women "learn the ropes" and further their personal and career development. Knowing the industry and being active in your field of engineering will expand opportunities for advancement.

ORGANIZATIONS FOR WOMEN IN ENGINEERING

Engineer Girl
National Academy of Engineering
500 Fifth St. NW, Rm 1047
Washington, DC 20001
engineergirl.org

National Center for Women & Information Technology (NCWIT)
University of Colorado
Campus Box 322
Boulder, CO 80309
ncwit.org

National Science Foundation (NSF)
4201 Wilson Boulevard
Arlington, VA 22230
nsf.gov

Society of Women Engineers (SWE)
230 E. Ohio St., Suite 400
Chicago, IL 60611
swe.org

CHAPTER

6

MINORITIES IN ENGINEERING

Contributed by Andrew Horn, Project Manager, The Rise Group

According to the U.S. Census Bureau's 2005 survey, people of color make up 25 percent of the U.S. population. However, only 6 percent of students enrolled in engineering majors are African-American, 7.2 percent are Hispanic, and less than 1 percent are Native American. Nonetheless, minorities continue to make significant contributions to the field of engineering and to society.

Did you know that the innovative body design of the Saturn SL I automobile was the responsibility of an African-American engineer? Did you know that IBM's Patricia Romero Cronin is a global expert in e-business services and integration? Did you also know that she was the vice president of Olympic Technology Integration in 1999? In that capacity, she headed all Olympic development activities in Spain and the integration of all software for the Olympic Games in Sydney, Australia. Did you know that a major research laboratory, funded by the University of California and the U.S. Department of Energy, has an American Indian Program and a joint engineering pact with the Navajos?

Even with the many achievements of minority engineers, challenges still persist. This chapter will examine some of those challenges and offer strategies for addressing them.

THE CHALLENGES

There are several challenges that people of color may face when entering the field of engineering. These challenges need to be addressed and overcome.

Although this trend is changing, there are still many young people of color who did not grow up with an engineer in the family. This fact defines the first challenge—exposure. When people of color become more aware of the contributions of engineers in society and specifically contributions of other people of color in engineering, it creates a greater desire to explore the field. We will discuss how to become more exposed to engineering opportunities in the next section.

Another challenge facing young people of color is not being prepared educationally. If the determination and discipline are strong enough, anyone has the ability to become an engineer. Unfortunately, the student may not reach his or her full potential in middle and high school if the appropriate study skills are not adequately taught. This often is through no fault of the student but is more an existing condition of the environment and the educational system they grew up in. While the motivation to study is increased if the student has a vision for his or her future, the study skills need to become second nature. These include turning in homework assignments on time, asking the teacher questions to further understanding, reading the book when it's assigned, completing the problem sets as best as possible, and requesting outside tutoring if necessary. There is nothing wrong with asking for help, and the most successful people are the ones who know how to gain access to the information they need to accomplish their task. There are many books written about how to develop adequate study skills, which can be easily identified on the Internet.

Finally, money is often a challenge. Although the cost of an engineering education is typically high, there are many scholarships specifically available to people of color in engineering, some of which can be obtained before entering college and some of which can be obtained while in college. Information about many of these scholarships can be found at the National Action Council for Minorities in Engineering (NACME) website, nacme.org. A lack of financial resources should never be a barrier to a person of color reaching his or her full potential in engineering.

There are a number of different avenues to become more exposed to the field of engineering. A simple Internet search can easily yield numerous high school summer programs geared toward introducing people of color to engineering. There are also organizations, such as INROADS and the ACE Mentor program, that expose high school students to careers in engineering and other professional development topics before they enter college. Many high schools or local communities host college fairs where students and their parents can learn about the different programs offered at specific colleges and universities.

Many colleges and universities have summer bridge programs specifically designed to help people of color majoring in engineering make the transition to college. These summer bridge programs help students create an immediate network of other students on campus that can develop into study groups and long-lasting friendships. These programs also help demystify the college experience by providing mini-classes, housing in the dorms, tours to on-campus resources, and introductions to upperclassmen, professors, and faculty as well as fun outings that seek to orient people of color to the institution they've selected. All of these experiences build confidence, which is a key component to being successful in engineering in college.

Throughout high school and college, extracurricular activities are highly encouraged. These will make you a more well-rounded student and give you valuable experience working with teams and developing social and leadership skills that will also prepare you for a successful college experience. In addition, extracurricular activities challenge you to manage your time effectively. Time management is one of the soft skills that is required for success in college and your future career.

It is best to begin researching colleges and universities as early as possible in high school. If you have an opportunity to visit the college or university, meeting with the Minority Engineering Program (MEP) director can be an excellent way to become aware of the opportunities for people of color at that institution. These directors can also put you in contact with the local National Society of Black Engineers (NSBE) or Society of Hispanic Professional Engineers (SHPE) president who can share experiences with you as people of color in engineering. Make sure to ask about what kinds of study groups are available as collaborative learning is essential to success in engineering. Similarly, it's best to start inquiring about scholarships as early as possible so that you can apply for as many as necessary to make sure you have the finances to attend the university or college of your choice.

Once you are in college, identify any additional resources that can assist your pursuit in engineering. The MEP director is often a single source for this information. Also, it is imperative that you visit your professors during their office hours—weekly if possible. This way you get to know them as people, and you become more comfortable asking any questions you may have. This can also give you a leg up in the competitive environment you're in as not all students will visit with their professors. Spending time with them in office hours will give you a confidence about your ability and demonstrate to the professor your interest in the subject matter, which often can result in a higher grade if the professor has observed you putting forth a strong effort to understand the material.

Engineering is one of the most demanding majors, but it is very rewarding and there continues to remain a need for the intellectual contributions of people of color in this field. To any person of color considering exploring engineering as a major or career, go for it!

ORGANIZATIONS AND INFORMATION

ACE Mentor Program of America
400 Main St., Suite 711
Stamford, CT 06901
acementor.org

American Indian Science & Engineering Society
2305 Renard SE, Suite 200
Albuquerque, NM 87106
aises.org

Minority Americans in Engineering and Science, Inc. (MAES, Inc.)
Publisher of *MAES National Magazine: The Magazine for Minority Americans in Engineering and Science*
11500 Northwest Freeway, Suite 200V
Houston, TX 77092
maes-natl.org

National Action Council for Minorities in Engineering (NACME)
440 Hamilton Ave., Suite 302
White Plains, NY 10601
nacme.org

National Association of Multicultural Engineering Program Advocates,
    Inc. (NAMEPA)
341 N. Maitland Ave., Suite 130
Maitland, FL 32751
namepa.org

National Society of Black Engineers
World Headquarters
205 Daingerfield Road
Alexandria, VA 22314
national.nsbe.org

Society for Hispanic Professional Engineers
5400 E. Olympic Blvd., Suite 210
Los Angeles, CA 90022
shpe.org

PART

TWO

Engineering Fields

CHEMICAL ENGINEERING

Chemical engineering is one of the oldest and most established engineering fields. Many consider it the central engineering discipline because it uses the engineering and scientific principles that underlie most of today's technology processes.

Chemical engineering has been described as "applied chemistry." While chemists are interested in the basic composition of elements and compounds found in nature, and some seek to invent new products from them, chemical engineers work to develop new products and to evaluate them practically and economically. Chemical engineering contributions have literally changed our lives. Chemical engineers have split the atom and developed recycling technologies and synthetic blood as well as catalytic cracking to make gasoline, plastics, synthetic rubbers, and fibers.

It is the chemical engineer who takes raw materials and turns them into new technologies and products we use every day. The jackets and shoes that we wear are most likely the result of innovations in synthetic fibers that chemical engineering has made possible. Similarly, some of the foods we eat, the cosmetics we use, and the stain-resistant rugs in our homes are the work of chemical engineers.

Chemical engineers combine the science of chemistry with the discipline of engineering to solve a wide range of technical problems, including finding more efficient ways of producing things such as plastics, synthetic rubber, medications, food, petrochemicals, and artificial organs. Clearly, the work of chemical engineers has contributed greatly to the quality of life that we enjoy today.

Some consider chemical engineering to be the most versatile of all the engineering disciplines. As a result, those who prepare to be chemical engineers are able to handle a wide range of technical problems. They are involved in every phase of the complex production of chemicals and chemical by-products.

THE WORK THAT CHEMICAL ENGINEERS DO

As stated, chemical engineers turn raw materials into useful products. In order to do this, chemical engineers know how to design new chemical compounds and chemical processes. They also know how to test new compounds and products to assure such things as their quality, durability, and manufacturability.

Today, chemical engineers use specialized computer technology for the chemical engineering field. They use this technology in their research as well as in the production of chemicals and chemical by-products. Chemical engineers also use computer skills to control automated systems in chemical plants and in manufacturing plants. Computer software skills are very necessary for chemical engineers who conduct analysis of research data gathered while developing new products and systems.

In combining the science of chemistry with the discipline of engineering, chemical engineers work on such problems as:

- Making more effective medications and medical devices
- Producing safer cosmetics
- Developing more efficient methods of refining petroleum
- Purifying polluted water and air
- Developing more durable and versatile products, such as plastics and synthetic rubber and fiber
- Harnessing solar and geothermal sources of energy
- Recycling reusable metals, glass, and plastics
- Producing cheaper and better fertilizers and pesticides
- Creating more effective paints, dyes, and coatings
- Manufacturing improved electronics and semiconductors

- Producing paper and pulp products
- Producing nutritional and convenient food products

To understand the nature of the work of chemical engineers, let's look at one company and see how their chemical engineers work. At Kraft Foods, chemical engineers can be involved in five different areas of the business.

- Some Kraft chemical engineers develop technology to improve existing products or to explore the possibility of new products.
- Some develop new products to expand the different types of food projects that Kraft sells.
- Others develop new methods for changing raw materials into finished Kraft products.
- Some engineers use their knowledge of package design to make sure that Kraft packaging will keep food products fresher longer, arrive at the store in good condition, and meet environmental standards.
- Some put quality and safety in place for both Kraft workers and Kraft customers. And because Kraft produces food that people will eat, Kraft chemical engineers who work in this area also make sure that Kraft Foods meets all requirements of the U.S. Food and Drug Administration and other government agencies, such as the Environmental Protection Agency, that help to regulate the food industry.

As seen in this example, chemical engineers perform many different functions, even within one company. The areas in which chemical engineers typically work fall into five general areas: research and development, design and construction, operations and production, technical sales, and environmental and waste management.

Research and Development

In research and development (R&D), chemical engineers spend much of their time designing and performing experiments and interpreting the data obtained. They may invent and create new and better ways of developing products, controlling pollution, reducing safety and health hazards, and conserving natural resources. Their findings may be refined in laboratories, but more often are tested in a pilot plant, which is a miniature version of the ultimate production facility.

Some R&D, such as that conducted by Kraft Foods, is done in the company itself. Other chemical engineering research is conducted in universities under the direction of chemical engineering faculty members with the assistance of graduate and undergraduate students. In all cases, research is aimed at technology development and a better understanding of the different ways in which chemicals can interact under various conditions.

Design and Construction

Some chemical engineers work in the area of design and construction. These engineers are also known as project engineers. They design and construct chemical manufacturing facilities. They may work directly for a manufacturing firm or for a consulting company hired by the manufacturer.

In design work, chemical engineers draw heavily on their knowledge of mathematics, physics, chemistry, and other related sciences. They use this knowledge to select and size equipment and determine the optimum method of production. Chemical engineers design computerized control systems to maintain consistent product quality, minimize waste generation, and assure safe operation of the facility. They develop capital and operating costs and present anticipated profitability statements to justify the proposed construction project. After the project is accepted, they prepare detailed specifications, drawings, and priority schedules.

Chemical engineers in design and construction can act as field engineers, directing and assisting workers during the construction phase of a project. After construction, these engineers may assist in installing and testing new equipment as well as training equipment operators. The most experienced chemical engineers will usually be the people responsible for actually starting up the plant and making sure that everything works as planned.

Operations and Production

Operations and production is yet another area in which chemical engineers work. Chemical engineers in this area are responsible for the day-to-day operation of a manufacturing facility. Their primary interest is to produce a product economically and safely in order to meet the customers' needs in both quality and quantity. These engineers are challenged by raw material variations and shortages, labor disruption, cost fluctuations, weather, and equipment breakdowns. They gradually adjust operating conditions to achieve improved product yield and quality and reduced operating costs.

Technical Sales

Chemical engineers also work in technical sales. Chemical engineers involved in this area not only have strong technical skills, they also have exceptional people skills. It is their responsibility to introduce new products to customers and to assess why some products do better than others in the marketplace. In the area of total quality management, chemical engineers involved in technical sales provide a vital link in determining why a given product is not functioning to a customer's satisfaction.

Environmental and Waste Management

Another area for chemical engineers is environmental and waste management. These chemical engineers devise techniques to recover usable materials from waste products and develop methods to reduce the pollution created during the manufacturing of a product. They also design waste storage and treatment facilities and pollution-control strategies for plant operations.

It is obvious now that chemical engineers do not work in isolation. Their work requires strong engineering skills as well as good people skills. They have to work with people from different disciplines and from different areas of the company to accomplish their jobs. Chemical engineers not only have to be technically competent, but they also have to be able to communicate with people who work in such areas as marketing, accounting, sales, and information systems as well as other engineering groups. This combination makes chemical engineering very rewarding!

WHERE CHEMICAL ENGINEERS WORK

Because a large number of industries depend on the skills of chemical engineers, they can be found not only in traditional industries, like chemical and energy, but also in industries ranging from advanced materials and biotechnology to business and finance.

While approximately 30 percent of chemical engineers work in consulting and government service, the majority of chemical engineers work in manufacturing industries. The largest of these industries is the chemical industry. Because the primary concern of chemical engineers is large-scale manufacture of products from raw materials through closely controlled physical and chemical changes, they find employment in such diverse areas of the chemical industry as agricultural chemicals, plastics, and industrial chemicals.

The petroleum industry also employs many chemical engineers. However, in recent years, chemical engineers have also been in demand in electronics, photographic equipment, pulp and paper, pharmaceutical, biomedical, cosmetics, and food-processing industries.

Other emerging industries for chemical engineers include the pharmaceutical, electronics, and environmental industries. Government agencies such as the U.S. Department of Energy, the Food and Drug Administration, and the Environmental Protection Agency also employ a large number of chemical engineers.

Chemical engineers work in local, state, and federal government agencies to advise lawmakers on environmental issues and industrial concerns. They develop laws and standards to protect the environment and the public from chemical hazards.

In addition to these areas, there are others. For example, almost one-third of the chemical engineers in the United States function as managers and supervisors and have become removed from day-to-day chemical engineering responsibilities. Others work for consulting firms, and still others teach chemical engineering at colleges and universities.

EDUCATION AND OTHER QUALIFICATIONS

Education for chemical engineering begins in junior high school with the appropriate math and science courses to prepare for four years of high school science, including chemistry and physics, and four years of mathematics—through trigonometry or calculus. In high school it is also necessary to take at least three years of English.

While the course work required for a bachelor's degree in chemical engineering may vary slightly from school to school, the American Institute of

Chemical Engineers (AIChE) states that undergraduate chemical engineering programs must include classes that provide a strong knowledge of:

- General chemistry
- Advanced chemistry (e.g., organic, inorganic, physical, analytical, and materials chemistry, as well as biochemistry)
- Materials and energy balances applied to chemical processes (including safety and environmental aspects)
- Thermodynamics of physical and chemical equilibrium
- Heat, mass, and momentum transfer
- Chemical reaction engineering
- Continuous and stage-wise separation operations
- Process dynamics and control
- Process design
- Modern experimental and computing techniques

Examine the course requirements in chemical engineering described on the websites of the seven different colleges and universities nationwide in the following list to see the similarities and differences at each institution:

- University of Arizona (che.arizona.edu/index.asp?ID=171)
- University of Florida (http://undergraduate.che.ufl.edu/curriculum/curriculum.html)
- University of Massachusetts, Amherst (umass.edu/ug_program-guide/che.html)
- University of Michigan (engin.umich.edu/dept/cheme/ugoffice/ChECurr.pdf)
- University of Oklahoma (ou.edu/bulletins/degree-sheets/engr/engrindx.htm)
- University of Southern California (usc.edu/dept/publications/cat2001/engineering)
- Virginia Tech University (che.vt.edu/undergrad_curriculum.php)

Chemical engineering careers in business, industry, and government require a minimum of a bachelor's degree in chemical engineering. Positions in teaching or research require additional college education at the master's and Ph.D. levels. Regardless of the work setting, chemical engineers need to continually update their knowledge and skills through continuing education courses and/or advanced degrees in order to remain current in their field.

OUTLOOK FOR THE FUTURE

Many factors affect future opportunities for chemical engineers, including the globalization of the chemical process industry, the increased sophistication of research and manufacturing, and the diversity of emerging technologies. In addition, there are fewer chemical engineers than any other group of engineers. As a result of all these factors, chemical engineers are highly sought by industry.

The continued demand for new and improved products and more economical processes will assure a steady demand for chemical engineers. In the manufacturing sector, the best opportunities will most likely be in the areas of specialty chemicals, plastics, materials, pharmaceuticals, and electronics.

Nonmanufacturing opportunities for chemical engineers are also expected to grow. This means that consulting firms, government agencies, and academic settings will continue to seek chemical engineers. As in the past, there will always be a need for chemical engineers.

EARNINGS

The U.S. Bureau of Labor Statistics reported the median annual salary for chemical engineers was $78,860 in 2005, with the lowest 10 percent earning less than $50,060 and the highest 10 percent earning over $118,000. According to a 2007 report from PayScale.com, chemical engineers with less than one year of experience had a median salary of $57,500. That means that half of the chemical engineers with this level of experience earned less than $57,500 and half made more. The median salary for chemical engineers with five or more years of experience was $73,100.

American Chemical Society (ACS)
1155 Sixteenth St. NW
Washington, DC 20036
acs.org

American Institute of Chemical Engineers (AIChE)
3 Park Ave.
New York, NY 10016
aiche.org

American Petroleum Institute (API)
1220 L St. NW
Washington, DC 20005
api.org

Independent Petroleum Association of America (IPAA)
1201 Fifteenth St. NW, Suite 300
Washington, DC 20005
ipaa.org

Society of Petroleum Engineers (SPE)
P.O. Box 833836
Richardson, TX 75083
spe.org

Society of Plastics Engineers (SPE)
14 Fairfield Dr.
Brookfield, CT 06804
4spe.org

CHAPTER 8

CIVIL ENGINEERING

Contributed by the American Society of Civil Engineering and Veena Kumar, Bovis Lend Lease

In recent years, there has been a decline in enrollment in civil engineering programs. Other disciplines, such as electrical or computer engineering, seemed to be more appealing because of their increased employer demand. However, the situation has changed dramatically. Today, there is a critical shortage of civil engineering talent.

According to a 2006 report to the board of directors of the Architecture Construction Engineering (ACE) Mentor Program (www.acementor .org), for every five people leaving the civil engineering field, one person is entering. As a result, the construction, architectural, and engineering fields are heavily engaged in programs to attract more young people to the field. They are also providing competitive recruitment packages in order to attract and retain top engineering talent.

While the current statistics are a concern, it means that those deciding to enter the field have a very bright future since in most areas of the country there are more job openings than qualified candidates. Therefore, if you like the idea of working on structures that can be seen relatively quickly and can improve people's quality of life, this is an exciting field to pursue.

Historically, civil engineering is widely recognized as the oldest and broadest of the engineering disciplines. From the pyramids of Egypt to the exploration of space, civil engineers have always faced the challenges of the future—advancing civilization and building our quality of life. Today, civil engineers continue to design and build the infrastructure—bridges, highways, rail and water systems, and so on—that supports almost every facet of our lives. In doing so, these engineers are meeting the challenges of pollution, traffic congestion, drinking water, and energy needs as well as urban redevelopment and community planning. To accomplish this they must be in the forefront of technology, making civil engineers frequent users of sophisticated high-tech construction products and the very latest concepts in computer-aided design (CAD).

Civil engineers offer the world answers and supply solutions for both new and existing problems. For example, earthquake codes were developed, in part, by civil engineers striving to improve public safety. Wind hazard codes are currently being researched and strengthened to ensure a safer quality of life for inhabitants of wind-risk areas. In 1995, civil engineers examined the blast damage of the Murrah Federal Building in Oklahoma City, to assure that new federal construction reflects the lessons learned from that tragedy. Since 2001, civil engineers have examined how the buildings, and their materials, performed during the September 11, 2001, tragedies at the World Trade Center towers and the Pentagon. Likewise, much research has been done on the failure of the levees in New Orleans as a result of Hurricane Katrina in 2005 and the Minneapolis bridge collapse in 2007. Investigations of these and other structural failures serve to educate engineers and make our world safer and more secure in the face of all types of hazards.

This profession extends across many technical areas, and civil engineering specialties interact with one another on a variety of projects and issues. Regardless of specialty area, civil engineers share a common denominator: civil engineers are problem-solvers who help people. They are responsible for serving their communities by improving the quality of life. Service to people and, specifically, to the development and improvement of the communities in which we all live sums up what civil engineers do.

THE WORK THAT CIVIL ENGINEERS DO

Civil engineers are involved in the conception, planning, design, construction, and management of projects essential to modern life, ranging from high-rise buildings to transit systems to space satellites to offshore structures, such as oil platforms. Therefore, they can alternately find themselves at a computer workstation, in front of a public hearing, or on a project work site. Most civil engineers routinely work as part of a team that may include other engineers, scientists, contractors, project owners, architects, bankers, lawyers, and government officials.

According to the American Society of Civil Engineers (ASCE), the oldest national professional engineering organization in the country, there are several specialties within civil engineering. These include structural engineering, urban planning and construction engineering, environmental engineering, transportation and pipeline engineering, and geotechnical engineering.

Structural Engineering

The structural engineer faces the challenge of analyzing and designing structures to ensure that they safely perform their purpose. Stadiums, arenas, skyscrapers, offshore oil structures, space platforms, amusement park rides, bridges, office buildings, and homes are some of the projects in which structural engineers are involved. These structures must support their own weight and resist dynamic environmental loads such as hurricanes, earthquakes, fires, blizzards, blasts, and floods.

Taking these variables into consideration, the engineer determines a combination of appropriate building materials that may include steel, concrete, wood, and other materials. If a structure must support a load and is made from steel, aluminum, concrete, or other materials, the structural engineer will ensure the correct combination of these materials is used to safely support the load. Then, to make certain that the plans are being followed, structural engineers are often on the construction site inspecting and verifying the work.

Structural engineers are team players. They normally work with architects, mechanical and electrical engineers, contractors, representatives of project owners, lawyers, public officials, and financial specialists.

Urban Planning and Construction Engineering

Urban engineers (planners) are concerned with the full development of a community. Urban planners use both technical and managerial skills to analyze the variety of information needed to coordinate projects, such as projecting street patterns, identifying park and recreation areas, and determining areas for industrial and residential growth.

The construction phase of a project represents the first tangible results of a design. Using their technical and management skills, construction engineers help turn designs into reality by applying their knowledge of construction methods and equipment, along with principles of financing, planning, and managing, to turn the designs of other engineers into successful facilities.

Urban planners and construction engineers team up frequently to build better communities. In urban and community planning, these civil engineers are concerned with the development of the total community. This involves consulting with local authorities on the integration of the community with mass transportation and other related facilities, and bringing the project in on time and within budget.

Environmental Engineering

Environmental engineers design and supervise systems that prevent and control pollution in water, on land, in the air, and in the groundwater supply. Their efforts are critical to all areas of water resource management, including the design of water treatment and distribution systems, wastewater collection, treatment facilities, and the containment of hazardous wastes. In this field, an engineer might be called upon to resolve problems of providing safe drinking water, cleaning up sites contaminated with hazardous materials, cleaning up and preventing air pollution, treating wastewater, protecting beaches, and managing solid waste.

The environmental engineer plays an increasingly important role in providing for the orderly growth of a community as well as for its continued quality of life. This becomes even more important as people move from crowded cities to what was once rural America. As people move to the country, so do industries and jobs. This influx places an increased demand on the public works of a community, so the environmental engineer's role as a planner and facilitator becomes even more important. Through the engineer's management and planning, growth remains orderly as the community expands to meet the growing needs of its citizens. The environmental engineer, by virtue of his or her mission, works closely with engineers specializing in construction engineering and urban planning.

Transportation and Pipeline Engineering

Transportation engineers are involved with the safe and efficient movement of people, goods, and materials. They design and maintain all types of transportation components, including highways and streets, mass transit systems, railroads and airports, and ports and harbors.

Transportation engineers apply technical knowledge and an understanding of political, economic, and social factors in their projects. They work closely with urban planners and construction engineers, since the quality of the community is directly related to the quality of its transportation system.

The transportation of gas, oil, and other commodities through pipelines has created another civil engineering specialty—the pipeline engineer. This specialty combines knowledge of hydraulics, geotechnical engineering, and the structural properties of pipeline materials to ensure a steady, reliable flow of these vital commodities. Like the transportation engineer, the pipeline engineer works together with the construction engineer, environmental engineer, and urban planner.

Geotechnical Engineering

Almost all of the facilities that make up our infrastructure are in, on, or from earth materials, and geotechnical engineering is the discipline that deals with applications of technology to solve related problems.

Geotechnical engineers analyze the properties of soil and rock that support and affect the behavior of structures, pavements, and underground facilities. In conjunction with environmental engineers, they evaluate the potential settlements of buildings, stability of slopes and fields, seepage of groundwater, and effects of earthquakes. With structural and construction engineers, geotechnical engineers take part in the design and construction of earth structures (dams and levees), foundations of buildings, and other construction projects such as offshore platforms, tunnels, and dams.

Geotechnical engineers are also involved in making precise measurements of the earth's surface to obtain reliable information for locating and designing engineering projects. Currently, geotechnical engineers make use of satellites, aerial and terrestrial photomapping, and computer processing of photographic imagery to most efficiently and effectively place and design tunnels, highways, and dams as well as to plot flood-control and irrigation projects.

Project Management

A career in civil engineering can lead to a position in project management. In fact, some construction engineers, surveying team supervisors, and assistant municipal engineers start their own engineering companies and take on projects that fit their expertise. Others join mid-size to large engineering management firms and manage large-scale projects.

College graduates also join construction management and contracting companies. Recent graduates generally start as assistant project engineers (APMs) and work under the direct supervision of a project manager or senior project manager. These APMs can be assigned to coordinate trades such as elevators, cabinets, drywall, doors, windows, and so on, or they can be assigned to the overall project, depending on the project size. Other entry-level assignments can include bid proposals, contracts, payments, resolving site issues, and coordination.

A related area is field supervision. In these positions, APMs work as field engineers under senior site superintendents and are involved with day-to-day field activities. These assignments provide hands-on construction experience and exposure to practical constructability aspects of a project.

There are a lot of campus recruiting events held by general contracting and project management companies that explain the type of experiences you can gain if you join one of them. It's always important to attend these events to learn more about the companies that recruit at your campus and the opportunities they provide.

In addition to the technical knowledge that you will bring as a civil engineer, project management positions also require the ability to organize and direct workers and materials, and excellent interpersonal skills. As these skills develop, so does the amount of responsibility the civil engineer handles, until eventually he or she manages larger projects that have budgets of millions of dollars. Interpersonal skills combined with well-developed communication and engineering abilities can give any engineer a distinct advantage when seeking a project management position.

Teaching Civil Engineering

Many civil engineers, after they have earned advanced degrees, share their knowledge and experience as teachers or professors of engineering. Beginning as an assistant professor, an engineer can progress to full professor or head of a department, teaching both undergraduate and graduate students.

Teaching is an especially rewarding way to relay knowledge that has been acquired over the years to prospective civil engineers. Due to their vast experience, faculty members are frequently asked to serve on technical boards, commissions, and other authorities associated with major engineering projects and research initiatives.

WHERE CIVIL ENGINEERS WORK

In addition to engineering consulting firms, federal, state, and local governments are major employers of civil engineers. Civil engineers can work for utility and oil companies, telecommunication businesses, and even toy and athletic equipment manufacturers. Also, civil engineers often work as consultants in their area of expertise.

The diversity of work and work settings makes civil engineering a dynamic profession. For instance, some civil engineers spend as much as 75 to 80 percent of their time outdoors. There are also opportunities that allow civil engineers to spend most of their time indoors.

EDUCATION AND OTHER QUALIFICATIONS

Entrance into an accredited civil engineering program may be at the freshman level following high school or at the junior level after completing an approved two-year junior college program. The typical four-year program of study in civil engineering includes one year of mathematics and basic sciences; one year of engineering science and analysis; one year of engineering theory and design; and one year that includes social sciences, humanities, communications, and ethics and professionalism, along with electives that complement your overall education.

The specific curriculum offered by different colleges varies. The exact information is listed in college catalogs. A list of accredited civil engineering programs can be obtained from ABET, Inc. (http://abet.org/accredited_programs.shtml).

A typical civil engineering program might include courses in the following areas:

- Basic science including math, physics, and chemistry
- Engineering and scientific programming, introduction to engineering, mechanics, soil mechanics, engineering geology, strength of materials, dynamics, analysis of determinate and indeterminate structures, hydraulics, and surveying
- Engineering design and design of steel and concrete structures
- Communications including English, speech, technical writing, computer languages, and graphics
- General education including history, philosophy, psychology, sociology, anthropology, art, music, and literature

OUTLOOK FOR THE FUTURE

Since the beginning of World War II, technological change in the United States has taken place at an ever-increasing rate. This rapid pace has produced changes in the style and standard of living throughout the world, particularly in the United States and Western Europe. Now, the infrastructure is a high priority. Without a strong infrastructure, the economy cannot continue to grow and expand. This realization and a need to rebuild and refurbish our roads, bridges, and buildings is creating a new demand for civil engineers. In addition, the pending baby boom retirement in the United States and the unprecedented population growth in Asia, India, and the Middle East are creating an increasing need for civil engineers.

While there are always shifts in engineering priorities that cause periodic changes in the demand for a given engineering field, there is now a critical need for civil engineering graduates. There is very little likelihood that this demand will disappear in the near future.

The types of activities in which civil engineers are engaged are critical to the continuing maintenance and improvement of the quality of life globally. Civil engineers focus on creating the infrastructure that surrounds and supports us. These activities range from the most fundamental, such as the supply of clean and pure drinking water, to the most sophisticated, such as the construction of space stations. The bottom line is that employment prospects for civil engineers are exceptionally good for the foreseeable future.

EARNINGS

In 2007, PayScale.com reported that the median salary (half the salaries are above the median and half are below) for a civil engineer with less than one year of experience was $47,000. For civil engineers with five or more years of experience, the median salary was $61,600.

Median salaries for civil engineers employed by federal ($76,000) and state ($63,800) governments tended to be higher than those reported for engineers employed by companies ($55,900) and private firms ($55,500). However, remember that in computing the median salaries, there are many very experienced civil engineers in the federal and state systems. Many are part of the baby boom that will be retiring in the coming years. This will no doubt decrease the median salaries for this market sector and pull it into line with that of companies and private practice/firms.

ADDITIONAL SOURCES OF INFORMATION

American Association of State Highway and Transportation Officials (AASHTO)
444 N. Capital St. NW, Suite 249
Washington, DC 20001
aashto.org

American Concrete Institute (ACI)
38800 Country Club Dr.
Farmington Hills, MI 48331
aci-int.org

American Concrete Pipe Association (ACPA)
1303 West Walnut Hill Lane, Suite 305
Irving, TX 75038
concrete-pipe.org

American Congress of Surveying & Mapping (ACSM)
6 Montgomery Village Ave., Suite 403
Gaithersburg, MD 20879
acsm.net

American Council of Engineering Companies
1015 Fifteenth St. NW, 8th Floor
Washington, DC 20005
acec.org

Coalitions and Special Interest Groups
Council of American Structural Engineers (CASE)
Council of Professional Surveyors (COPS)
Design Professionals Coalition (DPC)
Environmental Business Action Coalition (EBAC)
Research Management Foundation (RMF)
Small Firm Council (SFC)

American Society of Civil Engineering (ASCE)
1801 Alexander Bell Dr.
Reston, VA 20191
asce.org

ASCE Institutes (asce.org/instfound/)
Architectural Engineering Institute (AEI)
The Coasts, Oceans, Ports, and Rivers Institute (COPRI)
Construction Institute (CI)
Engineering Mechanics Institute (EMI)
Environmental and Water Resources Institute (EWRI)
Geo-Institute (GI)
Structural Engineering Institute (SEI)
Transportation & Development Institute (T&DI)

American Underground Construction Association (AUA)
8307 Shaffer Parkway
Littleton, CO 80127
uca.smenet.org

Associated General Contractors of America (AGC)
2300 Wilson Blvd., Suite 400
Arlington, VA 22201
agc.org

Association of Environmental & Engineering Geologists
P.O. Box 460518
Denver, CO 80246
aegweb.org

Construction Management Association of America
7926 Jones Branch Dr., Suite 800
McLean, VA 22102
cmaanet.org

National Association of Women in Construction (NAWIC)
327 S. Adams St.
Fort Worth, TX 76104
nawic.org

Project Management Institute
Four Campus Blvd.
Newtown Square, PA 19073
pmi.org

9

ELECTRICAL AND ELECTRONICS ENGINEERING

Have you ever wondered how doors know when to open for you or how your iPod can download and store so many songs? These are the types of questions on which electrical engineers work and find solutions. With more and more of our lives depending on computer technology, electrical engineers are increasingly in demand.

Our everyday life demonstrates the extent to which the work of electrical engineers impacts each and every one of us. Consider their work on satellite technology, global positioning systems (GPS), radio and television, computers and networking, sophisticated sensors and control systems, cell phones and PDAs, surgical and diagnostic medical equipment, wireless communications, and security systems. And, these are only a few electrical and electronic engineering innovations that have changed our lives.

Electrical and electronic engineering is among the largest of all engineering disciplines and seems to be the single area most in touch with today's world. From Wii consoles to remote navigational systems for unmanned helicopters, the work of electrical and electronics engineers is the result of both electrical phenomena and technology. Electrical and electronics engineers have significantly changed modern-day life and brought high technology right into our homes and workplaces.

According to the *Occupational Outlook Handbook*, compiled by the U.S. Department of Labor's Bureau of Labor Statistics, "electrical and electronics engineers design, develop, test, and supervise the manufacture of electrical and electronic equipment. Some of this equipment includes power generation, controlling, and transmission devices used by electric utilities; and electric motors, machinery controls, lighting, and wiring in buildings, automobiles, aircraft, radar and navigation systems, and broadcast and communications systems. Many electrical and electronics engineers also work in areas closely related to computers. However, engineers whose work is related exclusively to computer hardware are considered computer hardware engineers."

THE WORK THAT ELECTRICAL AND ELECTRONICS ENGINEERS DO

There are four broad categories in which electrical engineers work—power, communications, electronics, and control systems.

Power

Electrical engineers who specialize in the power field are involved in power generation, transmission, distribution, application, or a combination of these branches. They can work with different power sources, including fossil fuels (oil, gas, and coal), water power, geothermal power, solar power, or nuclear energy.

Power Generation. Power generation is merely converting energy from a static form to one that is adaptable to our needs. Engineers working in this field design systems that can utilize water power, solar power, fossil fuels, and chemical agents to produce usable electric power.

Geothermal, solar, and nuclear power generation offer some of the greatest challenges to electrical engineers. These power sources are considered almost limitless; however, harnessing and converting them to safe, efficient, usable power can be quite challenging. Consequently, electrical engineers who work in these areas require highly specialized training.

• **Water Power.** Hydraulics are used to harness water power by turning electric generators, called turbines, which use the water's motion to spin the turbine blades and drive the generators that produce the electric power.

- **Fossil Fuels.** Oil, gas, and coal are known as "nonrenewable resources" with particular problems of their own. Besides the problem of a potentially uncontrolled demand on an inherently limited supply, there is the overriding problem of environmental pollution that is produced when fossil fuels are converted into electrical power. Specialized electrical engineers handle both aspects of the problem.

- **Geothermal Energy Conversion.** The generation of electrical power from natural sources of heat deep within the earth's crust is experimental. Electrical engineers have coupled the conventional form of steam-driven, turbine-powered generation with some radically new technology, enabling them to convert the earth's core heat into a reliable and controlled source of steam power. This power will drive tomorrow's electrical generation plants. Though nonrenewable, geothermal energy can probably, according to the experts, be considered limitless, as a fairly large percentage of thermal energy is returned to its source.

- **Solar Power Generation.** Although used extensively in our space program, solar power has yet to achieve a cost-effective place in power-generation schemes. Converting energy from the sun to usable quantities of electric power is still in the experimental stages. Therefore, the future holds great promise for solar energy. Electrical engineers who specialize in power generation are working on more cost-effective methods of converting our limitless supply of sunlight to electricity to meet our future needs.

- **Nuclear Power.** Once thought to be the answer to our power requirements, nuclear power produces many problems for electrical engineers. While it is efficient, it has inherent dangers. Under carefully controlled applications, engineers have incorporated both efficiency and safety into the design and operation of nuclear power plants, which convert nuclear energy into heat that turns water into steam to drive turbines and produce electricity.

Compared to other forms of power generation, nuclear power is clean and relatively pollutant free. However, the way the power is produced creates unique and challenging problems for electrical engineers. Security— the physical containment of the nuclear power source—is crucial. Special techniques and controls must be developed to prevent and guard against leaks and equipment failures.

Electrical engineers designing nuclear projects must also plan for acceptable means of disposing of waste generated by nuclear power production.

This area of power generation requires the expertise of several electrical engineering classifications.

Transmission and Distribution. While electrical engineers devise efficient ways of producing power, others work at maximizing the transmission and distribution of electricity by more efficient methods.

The transmission and distribution of electrical power is governed by the strict rules of physics. There are power losses no matter how well a distribution and transmission network is designed. In order to minimize these losses and provide the maximum power transfer, electrical engineers design and implement schemes that utilize power transformers to convert raw electrical power to a high voltage for more effective transfer over long distances with less loss.

Applications. As power reaches its desired location, other electrical engineers have already been at work developing effective methods of using the power. These engineers specialize in power applications that can range from the design of lighting systems for major cities to schemes for the electrical motors driving some of the very latest rapid mass transportation systems.

These engineers must juggle several problems simultaneously. They must be conscious of the overall cost impact that technological developments will have on the end product and, at the same time, be energy conservationists, squeezing every last possible watt of energy out of a power source. These engineers also develop the machines that manufacture the products that make our lifestyle what it is. As such, they work in automotive engineering and paper and steel manufacturing as well as a host of other large and small consumer-related businesses.

Communications

Electrical engineers who specialize in the communications field are involved in equipment engineering, transmission engineering, switching and circuits, systems engineering, traffic engineering, commercial applications engineering, plant engineering, or acoustical engineering. Communications engineering has a direct impact on the production or operation of almost everything that touches our lives.

Electrical engineers in this branch design systems that receive, transmit, and deliver information in audio as well as video form. The radio, TV, and telephone are the products of electrical engineers specializing in communications. Recent technological advances, especially the joining of computer technology with information processing and distribution, have provided opportunities that once were only dreams to communications engineers. These engineers have made major contributions to military and civilian air traffic control, communications technology, and instrumentation used in space. The highly sophisticated surveillance receivers used in electronic warfare systems are yet another example of the type of work in the communications branch of electrical and electronics engineering. There are several kinds of electrical engineers directly involved in the communications process.

Equipment Engineers. Equipment or apparatus engineers are electrical engineers involved in the design and implementation of devices that take information and translate or convert it into a form suitable for transmission to distant locations. In essence, electrical engineers build the radio and TV transmitters and receivers that provide society with communications, whatever the form. These forms of communication include the fax machine, telephone, and computer-assisted technology that not only processes information but transmits it to a distant location where it can be used by others. These linkups also extend into space. Today, satellites serve as both transmitters and receivers, making worldwide transmission of data and images possible. Satellites act as relay centers high above the earth, linking distant points as if they were next door.

Transmission Engineers. Transmission engineers work with systems that include optical fiber, paired cable, and analog and/or digital equipment. They provide the pathways or channels for communications signals to be amplified and made reliable for such things as data and voice communications, including computer-to-computer data communications. It is very important for transmission engineers to thoroughly understand the science of wave propagation—the effect the earth and the atmosphere will have on a radio signal. In their work, transmission engineers design, develop, manufacture, market, and service products such as Internet hardware, navigational systems for ships, and high-frequency radios that require sophisticated methods of transmitting various types of information.

Switching and Circuit Engineers. These engineers specialize in switching circuitry. They are the control, direction, and "glue" for the entire communications effort. In addition, these engineers design and develop major switching centers in large cities and in the tiniest of computers embedded in medical devices. These switching centers are constantly monitoring the use and quality of communications traffic and transmission. If they sense an error, they reroute the communications with hardly a flicker or lost bit of information.

Switching and circuit engineers' tools include circuits, components, batteries, exotic power supplies, and banks of computers with programmed responses to rapidly changing conditions. For example, the impact of semiconductor and computer technologies on the telecommunications industry resulted in the conversion from analog to digital integrated information systems. This meant that engineers needed to have a strong knowledge of computer programming and systems analysis to program minicomputer-controlled systems for equipment used in industries as diverse as telecommunications and health.

Systems Engineers. Systems engineers specialize in improving the overall performance of switching systems. In general, they are among the most customer-oriented engineers in this field. They apply their technical expertise in support of the sale of complex technological products. As a result, they improve customer service by introducing new features and reducing communications costs. They typically

- Solicit technical requirements from customers
- Give presentations on and demonstrations of products
- Provide informal advice on what products might fulfill the customer's needs
- Write more formal documents such as proposals and targeted white papers
- Serve as a point of contact for nonroutine technical issues at major accounts
- Assist salespeople with the creation and execution of an overall sales strategy for an account

It is an interdisciplinary process that involves seven tasks:

1. Stating the problem
2. Investigating alternatives
3. Modeling the system
4. Integrating system elements to work as a whole
5. Launching the system to make sure that it does what it was intended to do
6. Assessing performance of the system
7. Reevaluating the system

Traffic Engineers. The traffic engineer, yet another member of the communications team, is the direct link between a communications system and its users. While the title "traffic engineer" might seem to refer to the movement of vehicles on the highway, here it refers to those engineers concerned with the availability of adequate communications services to handle not only the normal flow of voice and data through a system but overloads as well. It is important to point out that some of these engineers *are* concerned with the flow of vehicle traffic on streets and highways through the use of traffic light systems and electronic sensors.

Traffic engineers use a combination of engineering, planning, and accounting to perform their jobs. They study equipment capabilities and how to plot these capabilities against customer patterns of use. They study circuit operating efficiencies as well. Thus they ensure that a system can handle any demand without having excessive or unnecessary idle circuit time. They can be considered the "auditors" of the communications engineering field, assuring that all systems work as planned.

Commercial Engineers. Commercial engineers specialize in the service aspects of communications. This means that they study the public's needs for power and communications systems, especially the public's reaction to the actual services, the costs of those services, and any limitations that are of concern. These engineers are responsible for balancing rates (what a service costs the communications supplier) with revenues (how much the supplier can charge the user of this service). While some commercial engineers work for industry, many work for government regulatory agencies, where their knowledge of electrical and electronics engineering is valuable in setting and regulating government policy.

Plant Engineers. Plant engineers design all electrical and electronic aspects of a manufacturing facility. The work can include the design of generating plants, substations, and power distribution systems, but it also includes the design of state-of-the-art drive systems, digital regulators, motion controllers, programmable controllers, and microprocessors. Some plant engineers are responsible for designing the plant's computer system. Others are concerned with planning for the expansion of existing power and/or communications facilities and systems.

The plant engineer develops detailed studies that define the type and size of equipment required by the plant. They also oversee the selection and purchase of electrical equipment and supervise and support engineers from consulting firms that may be hired to design needed equipment. Plant engineers are responsible for starting up new equipment at the manufacturing facility.

Plant engineers also perform duties that are not usually associated with electrical or communications engineering. These duties include general day-to-day building operations and negotiating with local communities to secure land and rights of way.

Acoustical Engineers. Acoustical engineers specialize in the design and implementation of devices that convert sound to a form suitable for transmission over radio waves and then reproduce it through loudspeakers. They are concerned with the design of sound studios, theaters, concert halls, and other public facilities where people go to hear and see movies, concerts, and other forms of entertainment.

Acoustical engineers are also concerned with sound levels and noise pollution. Without them, what might be music to one person could be a source of pain to others. They constantly monitor the levels of sounds and formulate charts identifying what is a safe sound and when a sound becomes hazardous to people. Many of these engineers are also employed in industry to help ensure that workers are not subjected to dangerous noise levels in offices and industrial sites.

Electronics

Of the four well-recognized classifications of electrical engineering, perhaps electronics has the distinction of being the most visible and, therefore, the most "glamorous." There are many subcategories of electronics engineering, ranging from the mix of electronics and physiology (biomedical or clinical engineering) to computers and data processing. Along with these fields there are literally dozens of fields that affect our lives and our futures, such as consumer and home electronics, including digital televisions, radios, DVDs, CDs, and VCRs.

Electronics engineers can be involved in many areas of industry, including research and development; the investigation of new components and devices; the design of circuits, components, equipment, and computer programs; and the production of all types of electronic devices. In addition, these engineers advise on the materials required and cost of production of specific components or devices.

The shrinking of computer systems from room-sized machines to hand-held, and even implanted, devices has opened challenging opportunities for electronics engineers. The development and enhancement of electronic aids in air, land, and sea navigation have made travel increasingly safe and opened many new possibilities for electronics engineers. Likewise, medical electronics offers expanding opportunities for electronics engineers. Bionic replacements for body parts, artificial hearts, pacemakers (electronic regulators for failing hearts), and devices based on sonar are just some of the examples of biomedical advancements that are contributing to this growth area.

Control Systems

The control systems specialty deals with the analysis and design of automatic regulators, guidance systems, numerical control of machines, computer control of industrial processes, and robotics. Electrical engineers in this area are concerned with the identification of system stability, system performance criteria, and optimization.

Control systems are essential in the automation of complex manufacturing processes used in making products such as gasoline, detergent, appliances, food and medicine, and household items that are used every day. Control systems engineers design the devices that manufacture cars, cut out patterns in sheet metal, assemble parts, move objects, and control our environment.

Today, most home appliances have sophisticated control systems. Precision required in the manufacture of many electrical, electronic, and mechanical products is made possible by the control systems engineer. Together with other electronics engineers, they also produce machines to make other machines—or robots.

Related Fields

Many individuals trained as electrical engineers apply their knowledge to related engineering fields. A few of the common related applications are described here.

Electromechanical. Probably the most common merger of electricity with another field occurs when mechanical design is required to activate some new electrical device. Operation of the machine may depend upon some intricate mechanical apparatus without which the innovative electrical design is useless.

Electrochemical. Opportunities for electrical engineers in the chemical and allied industries occur primarily in the power field.

The chemical composition of materials used in electrical applications may be critical in some applications. To ensure consistent results, the electrical engineer may have to delve deeply into the chemical composition of materials. For example, for many years the presence of minute impurities in lead plates for storage batteries led to erratic performance. It was only through careful study and experimentation that unwanted impurities were weeded out and battery performance improved.

Manufacturing/Industry. Many practicing engineers move from their chosen specialty in a major engineering field to more general applications in industrial or manufacturing settings. With years of experience in an industry or in manufacturing, electrical engineers are apt to grow away from their electrical engineering field and move into the broader field of management, where their principal activities are in the management of a production organization.

Heating, Ventilation, Air Conditioning, and Refrigeration. It may be surprising to learn that heating, ventilation, air conditioning, and refrigeration can be considered branches of electrical engineering. Usually, they are associated with the mechanical field. Many electrical engineers have become interested in the electrical specialties involved in these disciplines and have gradually grown to embrace all phases of the subject. Actually, these are three fairly well-defined fields that are very closely related and can be combined to excellent advantage.

Heating and ventilation increasingly involve electric appliances for regulation, controls, and circulation. Electrical engineers also are interested in the possibility of solar heat installations and of storage of heat for equalizing winter and summer temperatures. These applications employ the same techniques as refrigeration. Hence the combination of refrigeration with heating, ventilation, and air conditioning comes as a matter of course.

Technical Sales. Many organizations that produce electrical or electronic devices or components employ electrical engineers in technical sales because these engineers have the background to discuss related electrical problems with prospective customers. As a general rule, sales ability is relatively well rewarded, and most engineers who enter this field remain in it, even though the application of engineering skills in their work may be slight.

Another sales opportunity for electrical engineers is known as an applications engineer. These specialists combine engineering and sales. For example, the manufacturer of arc welding equipment may require a sales engineer who can size up the requirements of a prospective customer, design welding equipment adapted for the customer's plant operation, and place the order in such a way that the supplier will be able to supervise, test, and make corrections where necessary for customer satisfaction.

Public Regulation. Work in public regulation consists largely of valuations of electrical plants and telecommunication systems, depreciation studies, and determination of rates. Knowledge of power generation or telecommunications is important, along with a good understanding of government and political science.

WHERE ELECTRICAL AND ELECTRONICS ENGINEERS WORK

The permeating influence of computers has greatly impacted the field of electrical engineering. There are now branches of electrical engineering that specifically handle computer hardware or software. Other branches rely on computers to enable technology for communication or for design and controls. This means that every setting in which electrical engineers work now involves extensive work with computers, whether that setting is in industry, consulting, government, or education.

Industry

Almost every part of the industrialized world's economy employs electrical engineers. The following is a partial list of the industrial settings in which electrical engineers can be employed:

Aeronautical/Aerospace	Food and beverage
Automation and robotics	Glass, ceramics, and metals
Automotive	Instrumentation
Chemical and petrochemical	Integrated circuits
Communications and telecommunications systems	Machine tools
	Medical
Computers	Mining and metallurgy
Construction	Nuclear
Consulting	Oceanography
Controls	Optoelectronics
Defense	Pulp and paper
Electric utilities	Textiles
Electronic and solid-state circuitry	Transportation
Environmental	Water and wastewater

Consulting

There are some electrical engineers who join consulting firms upon graduation, and they generally work in computer programming and software applications. But most engineers who become consultants usually have expertise in a specific engineering discipline and have practiced successfully in that field for many years. Experienced engineers in consulting organizations render complete services to their customers, including preliminary surveys, development, design, financing, operation, and management on large- or small-scale projects.

One phase of consulting engineering that has proved increasingly attractive is the development of specialty products. In this area, consultants start with the client's idea and work with the client in the product's research, design, testing, patent protection, manufacturing, and marketing.

Other consulting electrical engineers specialize in appraisals or rates for utility industries and government agencies. Still others may serve as expert witnesses in public hearings or in litigation.

Government Service

Electrical engineers are employed at federal, state, and local levels. Some electrical engineers work in such areas as military or civilian air traffic control, communications technologies, space technologies, surveillance systems, and patent applications.

Electrical engineers in the federal service are employed by such agencies as the U.S. Department of Defense, U.S. Food and Drug Administration, NASA, U.S. Patent Office, Bureau of Standards, and numerous federal commissions. Electrical engineers in state and local government service may work for many different agencies, but in particular regulatory agencies such as commerce commissions and transportation agencies.

Teaching

After graduation many electrical and electronics engineers go directly into teaching, usually at the college and university level, while others turn to teaching after years of successful practice. The teaching profession is very rewarding because it provides the opportunity to influence a new generation of engineers.

Teaching usually affords engineers time for research, writing, and consulting. Not infrequently, research undertaken in an engineering school leads to worthwhile inventions. In recognition of this, some schools have set up foundations to reward research that develops ideas and products for the benefit of society.

EDUCATION AND OTHER QUALIFICATIONS

In preparation for majoring in electrical and electronic engineering in college, the Institute for Electrical and Electronic Engineers (IEEE) recommends that high school students take courses in algebra, geometry, trigonometry, calculus, physics, chemistry, computers, electronics, engineering design, business, writing, and public speaking. In addition to the basic science and math that all engineering students take, electrical engineering students take required courses in mathematical logic and set theory, algorithms, numerical methods and analysis, probability and statistics, and operating systems. They also take courses in computer science and programming techniques. According to the IEEE, a typical undergraduate curriculum is listed in the following table.

Depending on the expertise of faculty members at a particular university, students then specialize in one of the branches or subdivisions of electrical engineering: power generation, control systems, communications, or electronics. Each of the professional societies in electrical engineering can provide a list of institutions offering academic programs beyond high school in electrical engineering fields.

Typical Electrical and Electronics Engineering Curriculum

Courses	Percent Time
Math	14
Physics and Chemistry	13
Introductory Computing	5
Mechanics and Thermodynamics	5
Electromagnetic Fields	2
Logic Circuits and Lab	3
Computer Architecture and Switching	5
Circuits and Electronics and Labs	13
Energy Conversion	2
Linear Systems	2
Oral/Written Communications	5
Social Science/Humanities	13
Other Electives*	18

*Electives may include additional technical courses in Semiconductor Device Construction, Advanced Topics in Computer Languages, Computer Architecture, Computer Construction, Communications, Microwaves, and so on, depending on the interests and the size of the faculty. Topics in business and arts and sciences may also be included.

OUTLOOK FOR THE FUTURE

As stated earlier, electrical and electronics engineering is a rapidly changing field. Because of its explosive growth, the job outlook for these engineers continues to be very good. Currently, most employers of electrical and electronics engineers cannot find enough good engineers, particularly women and minorities, to fill the demand. With the growing dependency of every industry on electronics, particularly in the biomedical industry, the demand for electrical and electronics engineers is expected to be very strong through 2014.

EARNINGS

In 2006, the U.S. Bureau of Labor Statistics reported the median annual salary for electrical engineers was $75,930, with the lowest 10 percent earning less than $49,120 and the highest 10 percent earning over $115,000. For electronics engineers, except computer engineers, the median annual salary was $81,050, with the lowest 10 percent earning less than $52,050 and the highest 10 percent earning over $119,000.

In 2007, PayScale.com reported that the salaries for entry-level electrical and electronic engineers ranged from $46,500 to $62,800. The median salary for these engineers was $55,000. The variation in salary depended on the level of education and experience. By the fifth year of employment, the median salary was $70,600.

ADDITIONAL SOURCES OF INFORMATION

Acoustical Society of America (ASA)
2 Huntington Quadrangle
Melville, NY 11747
http://asa.aip.org/index.html

American Electronics Association (AEA)
5201 Great American Parkway, Suite 400
Santa Clara, CA 95054
aeanet.org

American Public Power Association (APPA)
1875 Connecticut Ave. NW, Suite 1200
Washington, DC 20009
appanet.org

American Society of Heating, Refrigerating and Air-Conditioning
    Engineers (ASHRAE)
1828 L St. NW, Suite 906
Washington, DC 20036
ashrae.org

Armed Forces Communications and Electronics Association (AFCEA)
4400 Fair Lakes Court
Fairfax, VA 22033
afcea.com

Association for Computing Machinery (ACM)
2 Penn Plaza, Suite 701
New York, NY 10121
acm.org

Association of Energy Engineers (AEE)
4025 Pleasantdale Road, Suite 420
Atlanta, GA 30340
aeecenter.org

Association of Energy Services Professionals (AESP)
4809 East Thistle Landing Dr., Suite 100
Phoenix, AZ 85044
aesp.org

Association for Facilities Engineers (AFE)
12100 Sunset Hills Road, Suite 130
Reston, VA 20190
afe.org

Audio Engineering Society, Inc. (AES)
60 E. 42nd St., Room 2520
New York, NY 10165
aes.org

Electric Power Research Institute (EPRI)
3420 Hillview Ave.
Palo Alto, CA 94304
epri.com

Electric Power Supply Association (EPSA)
1401 New York Ave. NW, 11th Floor
Washington, DC 20005
epsa.org

Fiber Optic Association (FOA)
1119 S. Mission Road, #355
Fallbrook, CA 92028
thefoa.org

IEEE Communications Society
3 Park Ave., 17th Floor
New York, NY 10016
comsoc.org

IEEE Computer Society Offices
1730 Massachusetts Ave. NW
Washington, DC 20036
computer.org/contact.htm

Illuminating Engineering Society of North America (IESNA)
120 Wall St., 17th Floor
New York, NY 10005
iesna.org

Institute of Electrical and Electronics Engineers, Inc. (IEEE)
3 Park Ave., 17th Floor
New York, NY 10016
ieee.org

Institute for Interconnecting and Packaging Electronic Circuits (IPC)
321 Inverness Dr. South
Englewood, CO 80112
http://electronics.ihs.com/collections/abstracts/ipc-standards.htm

Instrumentation, Systems, and Automation Society (ISA)
67 Alexander Dr.
Research Triangle Park, NC 27709
isa.org

International Association of Lighting Designers (IALD)
The Merchandise Mart, Suite 9-104
Chicago, IL 60654
iald.org

International Municipal Signal Association (IMSA)
165 E. Union St.
Newark, NY 14513
imsasafety.org

Motor and Motion Association (SMMA)
P.O. Box P182
S. Dartmouth, MA 02748
smma.org

National Association of Electrical Distributors (NAED)
1181 Corporate Lake Dr.
St. Louis, MO 63132
naed.org

National Association of Power Engineers, Inc.
1 Springfield St.
Chicopee, MA 01013
powerengineers.com

National Council of Acoustical Consultants (NCAC)
7150 Winton Dr., Suite 300
Indianapolis, IN 46268
ncac.com

National Electrical Manufacturers Association (NEMA)
1300 N. 17th St., Suite 1752
Rosslyn, VA 22209
nema.org

National Electrical Manufacturers Representatives Association
    (NEMRA)
660 White Plains Road, Suite 600
Tarrytown, NY 10591
nemra.org

Optical Society of America (OSA)
2010 Massachusetts Ave. NW
Washington, DC 20036
osa.org

Power Transmission Distributors Association (PTDA)
230 W. Monroe St., Suite 1410
Chicago, IL 60606
ptda.org

Refrigeration Service Engineers Society (RSES)
1666 Rand Road
Des Plaines, IL 60016
rses.org

Robotic Industries Association (RIA)
900 Victors Way, Suite 140
P.O. Box 3724
Ann Arbor, MI 48106
robotics.org

Society of Manufacturing Engineers (SME)
One SME Dr.
P.O. Box 930
Dearborn, MI 48121
sme.org

Society of Motion Picture and Television Engineers (SMPTE)
3 Barker Ave.
White Plains, NY 10601
smpte.org

SPIE—International Society for Optical Engineering
P.O. Box 10
Bellingham, WA 98227
spie.org

CHAPTER 10

INDUSTRIAL ENGINEERING

The most distinctive characteristic of industrial engineers is that they are flexible. Industrial engineers figure out how to change things in order to do things better. When you are able to move quickly through an amusement park line, it is the work and design of industrial engineers. When you visit a friend in the hospital and watch patients being transported for tests and surgery, with a limited number of beds and wheelchairs, it is the plan of industrial engineers. When you order a new computer and specify the hardware and software you want and your computer arrives within a few days, it's the work of industrial engineers.

Industrial engineering involves design, organization, and implementation of integrated systems using people, materials, and equipment. These engineers apply their knowledge to a wide range of issues and in a broad array of settings. That is why industrial engineering is considered one of the top four engineering disciplines. In fact, industrial engineers are critical to the overall strategic planning of corporations, nonprofit organizations, and government agencies and often serve as the link between engineering and management.

Industrial engineers have always used their expertise to improve quality and productivity. In the past, this may have meant conducting worker time studies or designing a new facility layout. Today, industrial engineers use a "systems" approach to solving problems. A systems approach means that industrial engineers no longer study only one segment of the business.

Instead, they look at the entire process as a continuous flow of goods and information, and their primary responsibility is to improve that flow.

THE WORK THAT INDUSTRIAL ENGINEERS DO

Industrial engineers use their basic knowledge of engineering, organizational behavior, and the sciences to design, plan, and control production and service systems. They tend to take the "big picture" approach and use automation, computer-integrated systems, computer science, computer engineering, and information technology as tools to improve productivity, quality, and efficiency. They plan, organize, and carry out projects in a wide variety of settings. Because industrial engineers typically enjoy human interaction, they balance the needs and abilities of people with the availability and characteristics of materials and energy, as well as equipment and facilities. They seek the best alternatives to bridge the gap between management and operations. With this broad focus, industrial engineering has many facets.

According to the Institute for Industrial Engineering, industrial engineers become involved with such things as advancing manufacturing methods utilizing robotics; computer and information systems; energy management; financial engineering; facilities planning and design, including materials handling; human factors or ergonomics; human resources management; operations research and computer simulation; organization and job design; production and inventory control; and quality assurance as well as warehousing and distribution work measurement.

Industrial engineers get involved with such things as:

- Long-range planning and facilities design for a major transportation facility
- Robotics programs at a major automotive manufacturer
- Assisting in the design and installation of operations systems for semiconductor facilities
- Creating more productive workflow within a hospital or other health institution
- Designing a computer-based management information system for a financial institution

Industrial engineers are concerned with performance measures and standards, research of new products and product applications, methods to improve use of scarce resources, and many other challenges. Industrial engineers relate to the total picture of productivity improvement where productivity means getting the most out of a system for the least input.

Industrial engineers also look at the right combination of human resources, natural resources, and man-made structures and equipment to optimize productivity. They address the issue of motivating people as well as determining what tools should be used and how they should be used.

Industrial engineers are involved in such areas as operations research, applied behavioral science, and systems engineering.

- **Operations research.** In this area, industrial engineers describe complex systems in mathematical models to determine the best course of action to recommend to management.
- **Applied behavioral science.** This area combines engineering principles with behavioral sciences such as sociology, psychology, and anthropology to improve the management function. Industrial engineers study how organizations work and how they can work better. Their approach is scientific and quantitative. The management of technology has become a major application of this area.
- **Systems engineering.** Industrial engineers in this area are concerned with improving complex systems in manufacturing, transportation, housing, health-care delivery, energy allocation, environmental control, criminal justice, and education.

Logistics and Supply Chain Management

Expanding areas of opportunity in industrial engineering are logistics and supply chain management. Logistics is often defined as "the management of inventory at rest and in motion." Industrial engineers who work in this area cut costs, improve service, and boost profitability by taking a systems approach to focusing on getting goods and services to the marketplace in a timely, cost-effective manner.

Today companies are under constant pressure to reduce the inventory of supplies needed to make products and to decrease the number of products that are in their warehouses waiting to be sold. Companies must also eliminate wasteful and unnecessary steps in getting their products or services to market. At the same time, more and more companies are selling their products and services around the world. This has created global markets.

The creation of global markets means that many companies have a number of locations, plants, warehouses, vendors, and customers. Supply chain management focuses on globalization and information management tools. It brings together the purchase of supplies, the overall operation of an organization, and the process of turning raw materials into products and ultimately customer satisfaction.

Industrial engineers who work in supply chain management add value to products or services, improve the quality of those products or services, reduce costs, and increase profits. These industrial engineers work closely with outside organizations that supply their employer with the resources needed to run the business. They are very involved with the field of e-commerce and are knowledgeable about the most current supply chain software.

Using technical expertise and strong communications skills, industrial engineers in supply chain management become involved in selecting suppliers for their organization, negotiating prices from suppliers, and evaluating overall performance of company operations, transportation systems, and inventory and warehousing operations. They can also analyze the practices of the companies or organizations with which they compete for business to assure that their employer is remaining competitive in the marketplace. This analysis is known as benchmarking.

The five key issues for logistics and supply chain management engineers are movement of product, movement of information, time/service, cost reduction, and integration or cooperation within the company, between the company and its customers, and between the company and its vendors. When new solutions are found, the results for the organization can be significant cost reductions, a new competitive edge, improved products or services, and increased profits. The results for the engineer are opportunities for advancement, particularly to upper management and executive positions.

Executive Management

It has been said that industrial engineering can be a "fast track" to executive management. That is because successful industrial engineers possess the ability to communicate effectively and to manage projects and multiple tasks. To further develop these skills and abilities, industry is increasingly offering programs to prepare industrial engineers for management positions. For example, Eaton Corporation is a global, diversified industrial manufacturer. It is considered a leader in fluid power systems; electrical power quality, distribution, and control; automotive engine air management and fuel economy; and intelligent truck systems for fuel economy and safety.

Eaton provides a Leadership Development Program (LDP) within its Fluid Power Group for new engineering graduates. The program is well suited to industrial engineers because it targets graduates who want to move into management and progress to positions of business leadership through a fast-track career development process.

The Eaton LDP is focused on developing management skills through progressively challenging work experiences that establish technical expertise and provide cross-functional experiences and opportunities to develop leadership skills. It is a three-year experience with four to five different assignments selected to provide progressive work experiences, a variety of challenges, and significant career growth. The assignments are in the functional areas of engineering, operations, technical sales and marketing, and finance, and they include opportunities to gain experience in managing human resources.

Upon completion of the LDP, graduates have been exposed to Eaton's businesses and have worked in various functions and locations. In addition, they know Eaton's customers and understand their overall needs. Potential jobs at the end of the LDP can include to leadership roles in such areas as operations, sales and marketing, and product line management.

WHERE INDUSTRIAL ENGINEERS WORK

Industrial engineers can pursue their careers in a wide variety of work settings. Industrial engineering is performed in all major manufacturing industries. In addition to the manufacturing sector, industrial engineers are employed in such diverse areas as accounting, merchandising, banks, hospitals, government and social service agencies, transportation, and construction industries. The National Association of Colleges and Employers reports that a new recruiter of industrial engineers is the electrical and electronics manufacturing sector.

The airline industry, hospitals, management consulting and logistical consulting firms, and companies such as IBM, Caterpillar, GE, Ford Motor Company, General Motors, Eaton Corporation, Rockwell International, FedEx, and UPS are all major employers of industrial engineers.

EDUCATION AND OTHER QUALIFICATIONS

Mathematics and science play a key role in the industrial engineer's knowledge. At least four years of high school math, including calculus and trigonometry, plus three years of science, including chemistry and physics, are important preparation for an industrial engineering major in college.

The typical curriculum for a bachelor's degree in industrial engineering is focused, disciplined, and structured and generally includes two years of basic mathematics and science (physics and chemistry), introductory engineering, the humanities, social sciences, and English. In addition, there are two years of study in one of the following major areas of specialization in industrial engineering:

Decision analysis
Engineering economics
Human factors (interactions between humans and machines or
  computers)
Manufacturing systems
Optimization/logistics
Production, distribution, and material handling
Statistics
Stochastic systems

Industrial engineering is offered at approximately 100 accredited universities in the United States and Canada. A list of these institutions can be obtained from ABET, Inc. (http://abet.org/accredited_programs.shtml).

In addition to a college degree, increasing numbers of employers, particularly international companies and consulting firms, are placing a great deal of value on industrial engineers who hold a professional engineering license (P.E.). Holding a P.E. documents mastery of the engineering field and qualifies the industrial engineer to work on international projects and to lead engineering and cross-functional teams. The steps in the licensing process are outlined in Chapter 2. More information on professional licensing is available from the National Society of Professional Engineers at nspe.org.

OUTLOOK FOR THE FUTURE

As more organizations seek to increase productivity, reduce costs, and improve quality, the need for industrial engineers will grow. Every indicator points to an excellent outlook for growth in this field. Industrial engineers will be in great demand not merely because they are engineers but also because of how they apply their engineering skills.

The increased demand for industrial engineers is due in great part to the need for organizations to raise their level of productivity through careful, systematic approaches to production and to improve the quality of their goods and services. Even nonprofit organizations will increasingly use industrial engineers to sustain their position as useful service entities.

Because of the demand for industrial engineers, the profession is extremely attractive in terms of financial rewards. Organizations reward those who make them more profitable, and the industrial engineer does exactly that. In fact, salaries for industrial engineers are among the highest for all engineering disciplines, and many industrial engineers move quickly into management, making the outlook for continued personal and professional growth excellent.

EARNINGS

Industrial engineering starting salaries were strong in 2007. According to PayScale.com, industrial engineers with less than a year of experience had a median salary (half of the salaries in the survey were above the median and half were below) of $50,400. People with five or more years of experience had a median salary of $62,200.

While corporations paid a median salary of $56,800, hospitals paid a median salary of $62,400. These figures include industrial engineers with one to twenty or more years of experience and do not reflect entry-level salaries in these settings in 2007.

ADDITIONAL SOURCES OF INFORMATION

Institute of Industrial Engineers
25 Technology Park
Norcross, GA 30092
iienet.org

Institute of Industrial Engineers Blog
http://www.iienet2.org/blogger.aspx?blogid=588

Intelligent Transportation Systems, America
400 Virginia Ave. SW, Suite 800
Washington, DC 20024
itsa.org

International Society of Logistics
8100 Professional Place, Suite 211
Hyattsville, MD 20785
sole.org

Society of Manufacturing Engineers
One SME Dr.
P.O. Box 930
Dearborn, MI 48121
sme.org

11

MATERIALS
SCIENCE
ENGINEERING

Section contributed by Greg Geiger, The American Ceramic Society

Everywhere you look you see materials. Some are natural materials, like wood. Others are synthetic or man-made materials, like plastic. Almost every product in our homes, workplaces, and schools is made from different types of materials. The materials are selected to make sure the product performs as the user expects. For example, you want a jacket that keeps you warm but is also stain resistant. Materials science engineers work to make sure the polymers or plastics used to make your jacket meet both requirements.

To accomplish the goal of making materials that perform as expected, materials science engineers work at the molecular structure to change the properties and behavior of the materials. As a result, they make materials increasingly more useful. Where civil engineers design and build bridges that connect one side of a river to another, materials science engineers make sure that the molecular structure of the asphalt, steel, and concrete will withstand environmental conditions and the weight of the vehicles that cross the bridge every day. They specify and test the materials to make sure that those materials will not fail and endanger the lives of the motorists who use the bridge.

In addition to testing materials, materials science engineers work to make materials stronger, lighter, more durable, capable of withstanding high temperatures or low temperatures, and resistant to corrosion, stresses, and/or breakage. Many products are limited by the characteristics of the materials from which they are made. That is why materials science engineers work to create new materials. Their goal is to improve the performance of existing materials and products and to invent new materials and products that meet our changing needs.

An excellent example is the composite material that has replaced steel in many parts of today's automobiles. In addition to changing the design of cars, composite materials have had a positive impact on the environment because they decrease the overall weight of an automobile, increasing the gas mileage. Similarly, the materials in snowboards and water skis have enhanced performance and enjoyment of these sports. In many ways, materials science engineers play a key role in developing new technologies and new products because they deal with the production of materials that have properties that solve problems and are suitable for practical use.

THE WORK THAT MATERIALS SCIENCE ENGINEERS DO

All engineering disciplines require a good understanding of the materials involved in a product or process. That is why the specific discipline of materials science engineering emerged. It is devoted to the research and development of a variety of materials used in almost every industry. Therefore, today, materials science and engineering is one of the "in demand" engineering fields.

Materials science engineers are characterized by a high level of interest in physics, chemistry, and math. They use their knowledge of these subjects to study the properties of various types of materials such as metals, ceramics, polymers (plastics), semiconductors, and combinations of materials called composites. The work of the materials science engineer is focused on the composition of materials: how materials are made and/or how materials behave under different conditions.

In order to do this work, materials science engineers use a range of high-tech instruments and techniques. A basic tool of the materials science engineer is the scanning electron microscope. This microscope uses a focused electron beam to scan the surface of a specimen. Signals are generated when the electrons and the specimen interact. These signals are then analyzed to produce highly magnified images so that materials science engineers can deduce the chemical nature of the specimen.

In addition to the scanning electron microscope, materials science engineers also use scanning tunneling microscopes, atomic force microscopes, transmission electron microscopes, and analytical electron microscopes. All of these devices provide images of the most intricate details of the structure of materials so that the materials science engineer can better understand their properties and behaviors.

Materials science engineers use numerous technologically advanced techniques to study materials. Some of these techniques include rapid freezing or low gravity of space. In addition, they use high-speed computers to model the behavior of atoms, materials, components, and systems. These computers make it possible for some materials science engineers to create new materials without ever having to leave their desks!

Materials science engineers can be broken into five primary groups, depending on the materials with which they work.

Metallurgical engineers
Ceramics engineers
Plastics or polymers engineers
Composite engineers
Semiconductor engineers

Metallurgical Engineers

Metallurgical engineers work in mineral- and metal-related industries with various combinations of metals. This is a very broad field that encompasses minerals, metals, and materials processing and manufacturing. There are five types of metallurgical engineering: mineral processing engineering, extractive metallurgy, process metallurgy, physical metallurgy, and welding engineering.

Mineral Processing Engineering. Mineral processing engineering takes into account the differences in physical and/or chemical properties of minerals to develop, manage, and control the processes for separating and concentrating minerals in associated waste rock.

Extractive Metallurgy. Extractive metallurgy is the removal of metals from ores, concentrates, and scrap. Engineers working in this area use water chemistry, electrochemistry, and/or thermal chemistry technologies to extract metal from its sources.

Process Metallurgy. Process metallurgy is the development and improvement of processes that make metals and alloys into useful products. These processes include alloying, forging, rolling, casting, and powdering.

Physical Metallurgy. Physical metallurgy is the study of the nature, structure, and physical properties of metals and their alloys in order to control various chemical, physical, and mechanical properties of the metals and alloys.

Welding Engineering. Welding engineering is concerned with joining materials together, particularly metals, to produce efficient joints while ensuring minimum damage to the integrity of the materials being joined.

Ceramics Engineers

Ceramics engineers work with nonmetallic, inorganic materials produced from raw materials that are, for the most part, abundant and relatively inexpensive. They may also work with materials that are chemically synthesized and not available in a natural state.

To many, the word *ceramic* evokes images of coffee mugs, dinner plates, decorative pottery, tile, and maybe even toilets. While these are ceramic, there are so many other applications for ceramics, of which most people are totally unaware. In fact, some have called ceramics "the hidden industry" because even though ceramics are so widely used, most people do not realize they are ceramic.

Some of the industries that use ceramic materials along with a few specific uses are: electronics (MP3 players and computers); environmental (containment of nuclear waste, filters for harmful pollutants, and hydrogen fuel cells as a cleaner energy source); automotive (sensors, spark plug insulators, and catalyst for pollution control); nuclear (fuel rods for power plants); military (armor for soldiers, Hummers, helicopters, tanks, and trucks); construction (brick, tile, glass, and concrete); medical (bone replacement and imaging); communication (fiber optics and filters for cell phones); and industrial (cutting tools, wear resistant parts, and high temperature and corrosion resistant ceramics for furnaces, kilns, and other demanding environments).

The space program is a major consumer of ceramics. The heat shield tiles on the space shuttle, space capsules, and even missile nose cones are made of specially formulated ceramic materials. Closer to home, the cement, brick, tile, and glass used in the construction of houses are also ceramic.

Ceramics engineers work with materials having a wide range of characteristics that can be exploited in the development of new products. For example, ceramic materials that are insulating yet magnetic make the household microwave oven possible. Replacements for human bones and teeth that are durable, lightweight, and strong are also made possible by ceramics engineering.

Ceramics engineers have also produced new applications for existing products such as glass. Glass fibers are now replacing metal wires in communications systems. Telephone companies can transmit voices and data using laser technology and optical glass fibers. A major advantage is that more information can be sent through a relatively smaller cable.

Fiber optics—as the application of glass fibers in communications is known—offers virtually no interference and less resistance than is commonly associated with conventional metal cables. For this reason, many existing telephone lines are being replaced with cables made of glass fibers. This technological advance would not have been possible without the efforts of the ceramics engineer.

Two segments of the electronics industry, electrical utility companies and semiconductor manufacturers, also rely heavily on the skills of the ceramics engineer. Electric utilities require huge ceramic insulators for their high-voltage power transmission lines. They also use smaller insulators on the poles in front of houses or apartments. These insulators protect workers and the public from stray electrical voltages and also prevent the loss of electricity to the ground.

The semiconductor industry could not exist without ceramics engineering. Ceramics are used as insulators and building blocks for the integrated circuits, or chips, that have made so many of today's products possible and affordable. These chips are used in MP3 players, iPods, cell phones, PDAs, digital cameras, calculators, watches, stereos, televisions, and communications satellites. There are other uses and applications for integrated circuits and semiconductors, but it would be safe to say that without the ceramics engineer's contributions, we wouldn't have the standard of living or the electrical and electronic aids we take for granted.

Other electronic components also rely on ceramics engineering. These include capacitors, resistors, and modern sensors that convert information to electrical impulses for further processing and are used in control systems as well as in medical electronics technology.

Plastics or Polymers Engineers

Plastics engineers are engaged in the development, conversion, and application of plastics. The plastics industry is one of the largest manufacturing industries in the United States and plays an important role in such markets as packaging, construction, transportation, consumer and institutional products, furniture and furnishings, electrical/electronic components, adhesives, and inks and coatings.

Plastic materials are produced by combining chains of hydrocarbon molecules known as polymers. How the hydrogen is combined with the carbon and how these chains are strung together are challenges for plastics engineers. For example, some plastics engineers design and manufacture such things as thermoplastic compounds and specialty compounds for specific uses. Some make custom-molded plastics needed to package products for a wide variety of industries. Still others conduct research on and test plastics technologies and processes. The research, analysis, modeling, design, and testing of new plastics generally involves such activities as compounding, extrusion, molding, working with nanoscale structures, biopolymer engineering, and multiscale modeling.

New plastics have replaced more traditional materials, such as metal, glass, and wood, in a variety of applications, including in automobiles, computers, furniture, and packaging. Engineered plastics have revolutionized the world of materials, and plastics engineers are at the forefront of this development.

Composite Engineers

Materials science engineering combines several principles of physical metallurgy, ceramics, and polymer chemistry to develop new materials for a particular use or application. The materials science engineer integrates most, if not all, of the techniques of materials science engineering to produce these new materials or to make existing materials more useful as the needs of society and industry change.

Composites, as the name implies, are combinations of two or more different materials. For example, thin fibers of metals or nonmetals are literally woven into a fabric. This fabric is placed in a mold and covered with an engineered plastic resin. The result is a lightweight, strong, and durable material that combines properties of the base materials with corrosion resistance and flexibility. Often, these engineered materials are clearly superior to the separate materials that compose them.

The aircraft industry, the space program, and even the auto industry are making increased use of these engineered materials. The stealth technology by which an object is made invisible to radar, for example, would not be possible without composite technology. In this application, materials are deliberately selected that will absorb rather than reflect radar waves, rendering the object mostly invisible to the radar operator.

In other, nonmilitary applications, substituting composite materials for more conventional metals or alloys has allowed commercial jet aircraft to fly farther and faster, with less fuel, than the noncomposite aircraft of just a few years ago.

Automobile manufacturers are major users of composite materials, which are used to replace metals that are heavier, not corrosion-resistant, or not as strong. Reducing an automobile's weight by using these lighter composites increases its fuel efficiency while ensuring corrosion resistance and strength.

Boats, campers, and trailers are made of fiberglass, a composite material that is much more useful and durable than the traditional wood or metal products it replaced. Fiberglass is a good example of composite engineering brought to the consumer level.

Semiconductor Engineers

Semiconductor devices are essential in modern electrical devices. Materials science engineers who work in the area of semiconductors make sure that there is electrical conductivity between conductors and insulators in a variety of materials, where the electrical properties are dependent upon small amounts of impurities. The ability to control conductivity is the feature and makes the semiconductor useful.

Silicon is used to create most semiconductors, but more and more materials are used as well. Some of the products that depend on the work of semiconductor engineers include fiber optic cables, integrated circuits used in high-speed computer chips and CDs. Examples of everyday products that depend on semiconductor engineers are computers, cell phones, iPods, and MP3 players.

Nanotechnology. Nanotechnology is a new focus of many materials science engineers. It is the study and manufacture of structures and devices with dimensions about the size of a molecule. In fact, nanoparticles are only about a billionth of a meter in size—a nanometer. When these nanoparticles are clumped together, they usually have different qualities than materials made from larger particles. This is why nanotechnology has such great potential for the future and why the federal government has increased funding for nanotechnology research through the National Nanotechnology Initiative. Therefore, more advances in this area of materials science engineering are expected.

Technology continues to shrink microelectronics so that devices are on the molecular and subatomic scale. This ability has the potential to change manufacturing and improve the properties and performance of materials. For example, nanotechnology has the potential to have major impact on global warming and advanced medical technology. Specifically, nanotechnology has the potential to remove excess greenhouse gases from the atmosphere or to repair tissue such as skin or bone.

Other uses for nanomaterials include transistors, microscope tips, hydrogen containers, electron guns, and protective coatings for tools. In health care, nanometer-scale packages can control where medicine is released in the body. By so doing, high-powered medication only goes to those parts of the body that need it.

It has only been recently that the full potential of nanomaterials has been recognized. Therefore, it is expected that nanotechnology will create many new jobs and new industries for materials science engineers during the twenty-first century.

Job Functions of Materials Science Engineers

Whether materials science engineers specialize in metals, ceramics, polymers, semiconductors, electronic materials, or nanotechnology, they work in many different job functions. Some of these functions are research, manufacturing, applications, technical sales, services, consulting, management, and writing and teaching.

Research. Working with the building blocks of matter, engineers can unlock the secrets of nature. Basic knowledge is discovered that can benefit people everywhere.

Manufacturing. This field handles the production of high-quality, reliable, uniform, predictable materials. The materials science engineer is a vital contributor to this effort.

Applications. Applications engineers develop new ways, new processes, and new materials to make virtually any product. The materials science engineer helps a company by applying technology to improve existing products or to produce better ones.

Technical Sales. The engineer's skills in matching materials to products and products to applications combined with his or her communications skills make for the best of all possible sales representation. Thus, a materials science engineer can succeed where others might fail in the sale and marketing of products.

Services. Materials science engineers apply their problem-solving techniques and communications skills to help customers solve problems they have with products the engineer may have developed.

Consulting. Independent materials science engineers serve a variety of clients who have diverse needs. Many companies require the skills that only a materials science engineer possesses. If they do not employ materials science engineers, these companies must hire independent consultants. The consultant frequently provides the competitive and technological edge the company requires in order to expand markets.

Management. Engineers use a systematic approach to problem solving. For this reason, many serve as managers and supervisors, using their investigative skills to identify and solve a variety of problems, including the allocation of both material and human resources.

Writing and Teaching. Both writing and teaching build on communications skills and a desire to impart information. Materials science engineers can promote technology and train tomorrow's problem-solvers by teaching or publishing about their field and experiences. The ability to take a complex process, solution, or technology and explain it so that students can benefit is the mark of a true engineering professional.

WHERE MATERIALS SCIENCE ENGINEERS WORK

In today's economy, materials science engineers face the challenge of meeting current needs and developing new technologies in such diverse areas as medicine, food, energy, conservation, and pollution. Materials science engineers head many problem-solving teams charged with engineering new materials that will replace older, nonrenewable resources and improve our quality of life. In order to accomplish these tasks, they will be employed in the following areas:

- **Materials-Producing Companies.** These companies produce better materials more efficiently and cleanly and provide the raw ingredients to make the advanced machinery and equipment needed to solve other technological problems.
- **Manufacturing Companies.** These companies utilize the services of the materials science engineer to more effectively manufacture products such as cars, appliances, electronics, aerospace equipment, other machinery, and medicine. The materials science engineer plays a vital role in improving materials, processes, product reliability and safety, chemical processing, environmental processes, paper, plastics, and textiles. According to the U.S. Bureau of Labor Statistics (bls.gov), there were approximately twenty-two thousand materials science engineers employed in the United States in 2006. Most were employed in the manufacturing sector.
- **Service Companies.** All companies that serve the public's needs rely on materials science engineers to maintain safe, reliable service. Examples of such services include airlines, railroads, and utilities.
- **Consulting Firms.** These firms provide companies, institutions, and the government with independent outside help identifying problems in materials processing and performance. They also provide guidance

in developing practical, economical solutions to a variety of materials problems.

• **The Government.** Government is a consumer, promoter, and regulator of materials, products, and technology. It needs the materials science engineer to provide a flow of accurate information so that policy decisions can be based on facts, not political whims.

• **Research Institutes.** Institutes may work under contract to the government or private industry to probe materials, processes, and product development, ensuring that when tomorrow's products are needed, the technology will be in place to produce them.

• **Schools and Universities.** These institutions provide the materials science engineer with the opportunity to share knowledge and to train the engineers who will become the problem-solvers of tomorrow.

EDUCATION AND OTHER QUALIFICATIONS

Preparing for a bachelor's degree in materials science engineering begins in junior high school with appropriate math and science courses. It is recommended that future materials science engineers have three years of high school science, including chemistry and physics, and four years of high school mathematics, through trigonometry or calculus. It is also necessary to take at least three years of high school English.

College course work for a bachelor's degree varies depending on the institution and the specialization. Specializations and concentrations at the undergraduate level include materials, metals, minerals, ceramics, polymers, and electronic materials. In general, however, most programs will include two years of mathematics, science, and basic engineering and then two years establishing the structure, processing, and properties relationships for all specializations. Electives allow a student to develop a concentration in a particular specialization, and a sequence of two design courses in the senior year serves as a capstone experience for the bachelor's degree.

Many materials science engineers continue their studies beyond the bachelor's degree in order to gain more knowledge and expertise in one of the areas of specialization. They obtain master's and/or doctoral degrees. The master's degree usually can be earned within two years after the bachelor's degree. The doctoral degree usually involves six years of additional study.

Because much of materials science engineering occurs in the laboratory, advanced degrees are much in demand. According to the Engineering Manpower Commission in Washington, DC, there were about the same number of materials science engineers earning bachelor's degrees, master's degrees, and Ph.Ds. Few other engineering disciplines show such an even balance between undergraduate and graduate education.

There are more than eighty colleges and universities that award degrees in materials science engineering, metallurgical engineering, and/or ceramics engineering. A list of programs that have been accredited by the ABET, Inc. can be found at http://abet.org/accrediteac.asp.

The materials science engineering degree is extremely versatile; therefore, depending on career goals, some materials science engineers pursue study in such professional areas as business administration, medicine, management, and law.

OUTLOOK FOR THE FUTURE

According to the U.S. Bureau of Labor Statistics, "More materials engineers will be needed to develop new materials for electronics and plastics products. However, many of the manufacturing industries in which materials engineers are concentrated—such as primary metals and stone, clay, and glass products—are expected to experience declines in employment, reducing employment opportunities."

Increasingly, companies are contracting out their materials engineering work. This means that more opportunities can be expected in services industries such as engineering consulting firms. It is expected that other opportunities will develop as a result of the need to replace engineers who leave the field. Finally, discoveries in the areas of nanotechnology, superconductors, and buckminsterfullerene have the potential to create entirely new industries. These new industries will create more openings for materials science engineers.

EARNINGS

The National Association of Colleges and Employers' 2005 salary survey reported that materials science engineering graduates received starting offers averaging $50,982 a year.

For all other materials science engineers, the U.S. Bureau of Labor Statistics found that their median annual salary was $67,110 in 2005, with the lowest 10 percent earning less than $44,130 and the highest 10 percent earning more than $101,120.

ADDITIONAL SOURCES OF INFORMATION

Aluminum Association (AA)
1525 Wilson Blvd., Suite 600
Arlington, VA 22209
aluminum.org

The American Ceramics Society (ACerS)
600 N. Cleveland Ave., Suite 210
Westerville, OH 43082
ceramics.org

American Concrete Institute (ACI)
38800 Country Club Dr.
Farmington Hills, MI 48331
concrete.org/general/home.asp

American Institute of Mining, Metallurgical, and Petroleum Engineers
(AIME)
8307 Shaffer Parkway
Littleton, CO 80127
aimeny.org

American Society for Metals (ASM)
9639 Kinsman Rd.
Materials Park, OH 44073
http://asmcommunity.asminternational.org

American Society for Testing and Materials (ASTM)
100 Barr Harbor Dr.
West Conshohocken, PA 19428
astm.org

Concrete Reinforcing Steel Institute (CRSI)
933 N. Plum Grove Rd.
Schaumburg, IL 60173
crsi.org

Materials Research Society (MRS)
506 Keystone Dr.
Warrendale, PA 15086
mrs.org

The Minerals, Metals, and Materials Society (TMS)
184 Thorn Hill Rd.
Warrendale, PA 15086
tms.org

National Mining Association (NMA)
101 Constitution Ave. NW, Suite 500 East
Washington, DC 20001
nma.org

Precast/Prestressed Concrete Institute (PCI)
209 W. Jackson Blvd., Suite 500
Chicago, IL 60606
pci.org

Society for the Advancement of Material and Process Engineering
    (SAMPE)
1161 Parkview Dr.
Covina, CA 91724
www.sampe.org

Society for Mining, Metallurgy, and Exploration (SME)
8307 Shaffer Parkway
Littleton, CO 80127
smenet.org

SME-Affiliated Organizations
The Iron and Steel Society
The Minerals, Metals, and Materials Society
The Society of Petroleum Engineers

Society of Plastics Engineers (SPE)
14 Fairfield Dr.
Brookfield, CT 06804
4spe.org

Society of the Plastics Industry (SPI)
1667 K St. NW, Suite 1000
Washington, DC 20006
plasticsindustry.org

CHAPTER 12

MECHANICAL ENGINEERING

If you like to know how things work or how to make things work better, mechanical engineering might be the engineering field for you. Mechanical engineers design, build, and manufacture products and systems. Mechanical engineering is one of the most exciting engineering fields because of the breadth, flexibility, and individuality it offers.

While its roots go back to ancient Greece, mechanical engineering continues to be an extremely creative profession today. The work done by mechanical engineers varies by function and industry. Some of the specialties that mechanical engineers pursue include applied mechanics; computer-aided design (CAD) and manufacturing; energy systems; pressure vessels and piping; and heating, refrigeration, and air-conditioning systems.

In the manufacturing sector, mechanical engineers working in laboratory and field-testing arenas might test products as diverse as high-performance race tires and artificial heart valves. Those specializing in CAD, finite element analysis (a computer model of a material or design that is stressed in order to analyze for specific types of results), or mechanics of composites (advanced computer technology and material characterization to solve structural mechanics problems in composite materials) will determine the proper performance characteristics of the product's materials. For example, in the design and manufacture of cell phones, it is important to determine that the phone will not break if dropped.

In general, mechanical engineers take a broad outlook when solving complex problems. Mechanical engineers work in such areas as power generation, energy conversion, machine design, manufacturing and automation, and control of engineering systems.

Mechanical engineers hold a unique position in the engineering field because they not only design, develop, and produce devices for consumers, they also design, develop, and produce many tools required by other engineers to make products and systems. Therefore, their role continually expands to keep pace with technology. Mechanical engineers will always be vital to the success of newly emerging technology fields such as nanotechnology.

THE WORK THAT MECHANICAL ENGINEERS DO

Mechanical engineering is organized into three general areas: energy, manufacturing, and engineering design mechanics. Mechanical engineers are concerned with:

- The use and economical conversion of energy from natural sources into other usable forms
- The design and fabrication of machines to lighten the burden of human work
- Processing materials into products that are useful to people
- Creative planning, development, and operation of systems for using energy resources and machines
- Education and training of specialists, frequently called technicians, to manage mechanical systems
- The ability to be an interface between society and technology

The American Society of Mechanical Engineers (ASME) has forty-one technical divisions, reflecting the seven diverse disciplines, technologies, and industries.

Basic Engineering Technical Group
Applied Mechanics Division
Bioengineering Division
Fluids Engineering Division

Heat Transfer Division
Materials Division
Tribology Division

Energy Conversion Group
Advance Energy Systems Division
Internal Combustion Engine Division
Nuclear Engineering Division
Power Division
Solar Energy Division

Engineering and Technology Management Group
Management Division
Safety Engineering and Risk Analysis (SERAD)
Technology and Society Division

Environment and Transportation Group
Aerospace Division
Environmental Engineering Division
Noise Control and Acoustics Division
Rail Transportation Division
Solid Waste Processing Division

Manufacturing Technical Group
Manufacturing Engineering Division
Materials Handling Engineering Division
Plant Engineering and Maintenance Division
Process Industries Division
Textile Engineering Division

Pressure Technology Group
Nondestructive Evaluation Division
Pressure Vessels and Piping Division

Systems and Design Group
Computers and Information in Engineering Division
Design Engineering Division
Dynamic Systems and Control Division

Electronic and Photonic Packaging Division
Fluid Power Systems and Technology Division
Information Storage and Processing Systems Division
Microelectromechanical Systems Division
Petroleum Division
Pipeline Systems Division
Ocean, Offshore, and Arctic Engineering Division

In addition, ASME has six institutes.

Continuing Education Institute (CEI)
Emerging Technologies
Engineering Management Certification International (EMCI)
Nanotechnology Institute
International Gas Turbine Institute (IGTI)
International Petroleum Technology Institute (IPTI)

The Spectrum of Mechanical Engineering Functions

Figure 11.1 shows a list of the major components of mechanical engineering activities. This broad spectrum includes most of the types of work engaged in by engineers after graduation. In actual life, the graduate can shift from one activity to another. For example, a graduate can start in the production area, shift to the design area, later to testing, and then, in some cases, to technical sales. In small companies, one individual can handle several aspects of the business at the same time, as a designer, production supervisor, and testing engineer—all from the same desk.

As the spectrum implies, different talents and interests are required by different areas of the same company. For example, at the left end of the spectrum are engineers who are science-oriented, technically competent, and mathematically gifted. If those engineers consult or teach, they must also be able to deal with people and have skill in communicating ideas.

At the right-hand side of the spectrum are engineers who deal with materials, business matters, and people. Those involved as manufacturers' representatives or sales engineers or with legal aspects of engineering and business might not require the technical competence of a research engineer but should be knowledgeable about business, accounting, economics, and people.

Figure 11.1 Spectrum of activities engaged in by Mechanical Engineers

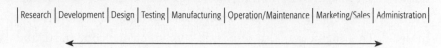

| Research | Development | Design | Testing | Manufacturing | Operation/Maintenance | Marketing/Sales | Administration |

In a spectrum of this sort, there is no higher or lower order. The left side is no more preferred than the right side.

Research. Research is the first step in solving a problem. The engineer will obtain data, devise new methods of calculation, and acquire new knowledge.

Development. In development, the engineer takes the information and knowledge gained from the research and begins to expand it. At this stage, a simulation or experimental device might be produced and further extended into either a process or system that approximates a solution to the problem and fits the final need.

Design. In the design phase, the engineer actually conceptualizes the machine, the approach, or the system that will solve the problem. Careful documentation of all details is necessary to bring the solution from idea to reality. The solution is described quantitatively and put into equations or CAD form.

Testing. To perform a test, the engineer will utilize either experimental devices or full-scale completed machines, systems, or equipment. These devices will be operated to determine performance. At the same time, the mechanical engineer is checking to determine how much use or abuse the device can withstand, its relative strengths and weaknesses, and how to improve its performance. In essence, this phase of the mechanical engineer's work is to determine that whatever is being tested will perform as it is intended and can function in the environmental conditions that were anticipated in the design criteria.

Manufacturing. In the manufacturing stage the mechanical engineer must answer a series of questions: How is the product best manufactured? What is the most economical way of making it? What processes will be required? What are the skills and personnel needed to produce it? These questions are answered by a production engineer, the person who selects the equipment and machines and supervises arrangement and operation in detail. This engineer is also responsible for efficient, economical, and safe manufacturing.

Operation and Maintenance. Some equipment or systems require specialized knowledge and expertise beyond the level technicians usually have for operation and maintenance. These systems and equipment require the continual care only a mechanical engineer can provide. These duties might be mandated by law, as are the supervision and maintenance responsibilities for a nuclear or fossil fuel plant. Federal and state regulations require a mechanical engineer at such plants to perform certain specific tasks.

Marketing and Sales. When a firm offers a complex product or system, it can't rely only on a salesperson to present it to prospective clients. This is especially true in the case of systems and equipment that require formal technical backgrounds in order to understand and explain them. In this case, mechanical engineers function as sales or marketing engineers, relying on their technical background and communications skills to demonstrate a product or a system to a customer. Often these engineers work with the customer to modify the basic system or product design to meet the customer's specific requirement.

Administration and Management. As in other engineering disciplines, administration and management are logical stepping-stones for mechanical engineers. As engineers gain more experience and show an aptitude for supervising and coordinating activities and people, they gradually find themselves with more people to supervise and more responsibilities. At this point, the day-to-day technical aspects of the job are replaced with human problems. The engineer will be formulating policy and guiding, coordinating, and interacting with people more than machines.

The preceding descriptions are not intended to be complete, but rather to give a summary of the sorts of things mechanical engineers do.

Mechanical engineering demands an aptitude for and interest in the physical sciences and mathematics, and it requires the ability to apply these interests to benefit society and meet its needs.

There are more than 225,000 mechanical engineers, and almost half of them are employed in the manufacturing sector. In fact, all large industries employ mechanical engineers. Traditional industries for mechanical engineers are the automotive, industrial machinery, utilities, chemical, computer, manufacturing, mining, and petroleum industries. However, mechanical engineers are also employed in such industries as publishing and printing, oceanography, textiles, pharmaceuticals, apparel, soap and cosmetics, electronics, paper and wood products, and rubber and glass.

Some other areas of employment for mechanical engineers include materials, pollution control, electronic packaging, medicine, and aerospace. In addition, mechanical engineers do research and teach at colleges and universities. They also work at the federal, state, and local government levels and for consulting engineering firms. Some employers of mechanical engineers include:

Bechtel Corporation	Honeywell
Caterpillar	John Deere
Chrysler	NASA
Dell	Navistar International
Eaton Corporation	Corporation
Ford Motor Company	Raytheon
GE	U.S. Food and Drug
General Motors	Administration
Goodyear Tire and Rubber	

EDUCATION AND OTHER QUALIFICATIONS

The American Society of Mechanical Engineers (ASME) recommends that high school students who are interested in majoring in mechanical engineering in college follow the curriculum recommended by JETS. These courses include algebra I and II, geometry, trigonometry, and calculus. It is also important to take as many science courses as possible, which should include biology, chemistry, and physics. English, social studies, and foreign language courses are all necessary preparation for majoring in mechanical engineering. Computer, economics, history, and public speaking courses are also highly recommended. Mechanical engineers follow a very traditional engineering education process at the undergraduate level. Courses include the following:

- Basic science including mathematics, physics, and life science provide a foundation for all engineering and technical courses.
- Engineering sciences with courses including solid mechanics, fluid mechanics, thermodynamics, heat transfer, finite element analysis, systems and controls, materials, electricity, and magnetism. In addition, some course work might be offered or required in the electrical and material engineering fields.
- Design manufacturing courses provide an introduction to the process of joining ideas, imagination, and modeling to create components and systems.
- Communications courses include English, graphics, and computer languages.
- Humanities includes courses from one or more of the following: literature, sociology, history, psychology, economics, and philosophy. These courses are designed to round out engineers and better prepare them for their roles in society through knowledge and understanding of their culture, themselves, and one another.

OUTLOOK FOR THE FUTURE

According to the U.S. Bureau of Labor Statistics, the demand for improved machinery, machine tools, and complex manufacturing processes is creating a growing demand for mechanical engineers. In addition, new areas such as nanotechnology, microelectromechancial systems, and bioengineering are creating opportunities for mechanical engineers.

Other opportunities are expected to be in the engineering services area (engineering consulting firms) as manufacturing companies contract out design, development, and testing work to solve engineering problems. According to the Bureau of Labor Statistics (bls.gov), this area is expected to grow through 2016. In addition, as the workforce ages and engineers retire, additional opportunities for mechanical engineers will be created.

Mechanical engineers had a median annual salary of $69,850 in 2006, according to the U.S. Bureau of Labor Statistics. This means that half of all mechanical engineers earned more and half earned less. The lowest 10 percent of mechanical engineers earned less than $45,170, and the highest 10 percent earned more than $104,900.

In 2007 PayScale.com reported that mechanical engineers with less than one year of experience earned a median salary of $52,415. Those with five to nine years of experience earned a median salary of $64, 917.

ADDITIONAL SOURCES OF INFORMATION

Air-Conditioning and Refrigeration Institute (ARI)
4100 North Fairfax Dr., Suite 200
Arlington, VA 22203
ari.org

American Boiler Manufacturers Association (ABMA)
8221 Old Courthouse Rd., Suite 207
Vienna, VA 22182
abma.com

American Council of Engineering Companies (ACEC)
1015 Fifteenth St. NW, 8th Floor
Washington, DC 20005
acec.org

American Design Drafting Association (ADDA)
105 E. Main St.
Newbern, TN 38059
adda.org

American Nuclear Society (ANS)
555 N. Kensington Ave.
LaGrange Park, IL 60526
ans.org

American Society of Body Engineers (ASBE)
P.O. Box 80363
Rochester, MI 48308
asbe.com

American Society of Heating, Refrigerating, and Air-Conditioning
    Engineers (ASHRAE)
1791 Tullie Circle NE
Atlanta, GA 30329
ashrae.org

American Society of Mechanical Engineers (ASME)
Three Park Ave.
New York, NY 10016
asme.org

American Society for Nondestructive Testing (ASNT)
1711 Arlingate Lane
P.O. Box 28518
Columbus, OH 43228
asnt.org

Mechanical Contractors Association of America, Inc. (MCAA)
1385 Picard Dr.
Rockville, MD 20850
mcaa.org

Robotic Industries Association (RIA)
900 Victors Way
P.O. Box 3724
Ann Arbor, MI 48106
robotics.org

Sheet Metal and Air Conditioning Contractors National Association
    (SMACNA)
4201 Lafayette Center Dr.
Chantilly, VA 20151
smacna.org

Society for the Advancement of Material and Process Engineering
    (SAMPE)
1161 Parkvicw Dr.
Covina, CA 91724
sampe.org

Society of Automotive Engineers, Inc. (SAE)
400 Commonwealth Dr.
Warrendale, PA 15096
sae.org

Society of Manufacturing Engineers (SME)
One SME Dr.
P.O. Box 930
Dearborn, MI 48121
sme.org

CHAPTER 13

AEROSPACE ENGINEERING

Contributed by the American Institute of Aeronautics and
Astronautics, Inc.

It seems humans have always been interested in flight. Leonardo da Vinci drew "flying machines" as early as the 1400s, and, in 1903, Orville and Wilbur Wright flew the first airplane at Kitty Hawk, North Carolina. In a forward-thinking move, the University of Michigan offered the first U.S. collegiate program for the study of aeronautical engineering in the 1920s. In the 1960s, President Kennedy committed the United States to going to the moon and back within a decade. All of these events have contributed to the emergence of a field that, today, employs more than 90,000 aerospace engineers.

Aerospace engineering, like the entire field of aerospace, has grown far beyond its original concerns with aeronautics and space. Aerospace professionals confront many challenges and even address problems closer to earth in the areas of mass transportation, environmental pollution, and medical science. That is why it is possible to prepare for a career in aerospace engineering either by pursuing a degree in mechanical, electrical, chemical, or materials science engineering or by pursuing aerospace engineering as a college major in its own right. Whichever educational path is chosen, aerospace engineers find themselves on the leading edge of technology, and their solutions to problems encountered in exploring space also provide solutions to problems closer to home.

THE WORK THAT AEROSPACE ENGINEERS DO

By definition, the aerospace engineer is involved in all phases of research and development in aeronautics and astronautics. An aeronautical engineer works specifically with aircraft, spacecraft, or aeronautics.

As technology races forward, the industry that once built aircraft and then spacecraft, such as the space shuttle, is now building aerospace craft, such as the orbital space plane. Thus, two interrelated industries are merging into one mature "aerospace" industry.

Aerospace engineering involves about seven major divisions—each with its supporting technology—that often cross the lines of other engineering fields. These major divisions include propulsion, fluid mechanics, thermodynamics, structures, celestial mechanics, acoustics, and guidance and control.

Propulsion

The study of propulsion involves the analysis of matter as it flows through various devices such as combustion chambers, diffusers, nozzles, and turbochargers. A vehicle's propulsion system is the primary force responsible for performance.

Fluid Mechanics

Fluid mechanics deals with the motion of gases and liquids as well as with the effects of the motion on bodies in the medium. Engineers working in the division of fluid dynamics called aerodynamics are concerned with determining a vehicle's optimum shape and configuration.

Thermodynamics

The science of thermodynamics is concerned with the relationship between heat and work. The principles of thermodynamics interest aerospace engineers studying thermal balance within vehicles, thermal effects produced by high-speed reentry into the atmosphere, and environmental control systems.

Structures

The science of structures develops advanced techniques in the areas of structural analysis, dynamic loads, aeroelasticity, and design criteria. The engineer in this field must answer two questions about any framework:

- Is it strong enough to withstand the loads applied to it?
- Is it stiff enough to avoid excessive deformation and deflections?

Celestial Mechanics

The science of celestial mechanics is concerned with the motion of particles in space. These particles can represent rockets, planets, missiles, or spacecraft. When engineers prepare a space mission, a major concern is determining the paths of the rockets and planets. Their calculations, facilitated by banks of computer devices, take into consideration the propulsion systems, optimum programs for fuel or propellant utilization, optimal trajectories, transfer orbits, and the potential effects of thrust misalignment.

Acoustics

The study of acoustics deals with the production and behavior of sound. Some of the problems aerospace engineers address include internal noise generated from stators, rotors, fans, and combustion chambers. They also study sonic booms and their effects on the urban and rural environment.

Guidance and Control

Guidance and control systems automate the control, maneuverability, and path systems of a space vehicle in order to fulfill its mission objectives. Examples of systems on a more conventional level include the instrument landing system (ILS), which permits aircraft to land day or night in all kinds of weather. Similar systems also provide guidance and control for submarines.

WHERE AEROSPACE ENGINEERS WORK

The settings in which aerospace engineers work vary widely. The environment could be an office, a laboratory, an airfield, or even outer space, depending on the career goals and interests of an individual.

Aerospace engineers who do cost analysis, preliminary design, or pure research would most likely work in an office or library. However, if an aerospace engineer were doing flight-testing, actual design, or field service, he or she would probably be in a laboratory or out "in the field." If an engineer were doing work on or for satellites, space shuttles, or the International

Space Station, then space could very well be his or her work atmosphere from time to time.

Many aerospace engineers are employed in the aerospace industries, including companies such as:

Aerospace Corporation	ITT Industries, Inc.
BAE Systems	Lockheed Martin Corporation
The Boeing Company	Northrop Grumman
Bombardier, Inc.	Corporation
Eaton Corporation	Pratt & Whitney
General Dynamics Corporation	Raytheon Company
Goodrich Corporation	Teledyne Technologies
Honeywell International, Inc.	

Many of these companies receive major contracts from the U.S. Department of Defense and commercial airline companies. Other aerospace engineers are employed in government agencies, particularly the U.S. Department of Defense and National Aeronautics and Space Administration (NASA).

EDUCATION AND OTHER QUALIFICATIONS

Experts agree that junior high school is the best time to begin planning for a career in aerospace engineering. Most colleges and universities offering programs in aerospace engineering expect the students they admit to have taken these courses in high school:

- English. Foreign students may be allowed to take an English class while attending school, but will most likely be expected to take the Test of English as a Foreign Language (TOEFL) exam.
- History. Three years including social studies.
- Math. Algebra, geometry, trigonometry. Most universities will start with a calculus class freshman year—if your high school offers calculus, take it.
- Science. Biology, chemistry, and physics.

A few high schools even offer aerospace engineering courses to students who excel in math and science. In addition, many high schools offer advanced placement (AP) classes. Anyone intending to major in engineering, especially aerospace engineering, should attempt to take as many AP classes as possible.

Many colleges vary in their curricula, but most will expect an aeronautics/astronautics (aero/astro) student to take the following classes (some schools do not offer an aero/astro degree, but have tracks within the mechanical engineering department to prepare students to enter the aero/astro field):

- Aerodynamics/fluid flow
- Basic sciences. Physics and laboratory [two years], chemistry and laboratory.
- Electronics. Introduction.
- English. English is the official language of scientists. Almost every technical or science conference will have the presentations given in English.
- Heat transfer
- Material sciences
- Math. Analytical geometry, calculus [two years], matrices and nonlinear algebra, linear and nonlinear differential equations.
- Statics and dynamics. Study of any and all forces on systems or objects that are stationary [statics] or moving [dynamics].
- Structural analysis
- Technical writing

In addition to these basics, students are expected to take several technical electives. Some of these can be on any technical topic, but three to four technical electives will be specific to aero/astro.

Some of these technical electives are:

- Orbital mechanics
- Electromagnetic fields
- Flight mechanics
- Flight vehicle design
- Gas dynamics

- Propulsion
- Space structures
- Spacecraft design
- Telecommunications
- Trajectory dynamics
- Vehicle stability and control

Special Programs to Explore Aerospace Engineering Careers While in School

There are many opportunities for students to enhance their education with other activities. One way is by taking part in cooperative engineering education (co-op). Many colleges and universities offer co-ops and often have an office dedicated to it. In fact, many schools are beginning to require students to do co-ops. The American Institute of Aeronautics and Astronautics (AIAA) website, aiaa.org, links to other websites that offer co-ops and internships.

NASA also offers several programs to help students, including co-ops as well as a variety of competitions. Some of the NASA competitions allow students the opportunity to fly on the KC-135A, also known as the Vomit Comet. The KC-135A flies a series of parabolic patterns that allow students to perform experiments in zero or microgravity.

The AIAA has student branches at more than 150 universities throughout the world. These student branches often have many local activities to help enhance aerospace education. Activities include local speakers from AIAA professional sections, mentoring with local high schools and elementary schools, and trips to and tours of aerospace industries. The student branches also take part in a regional student conference.

Regional student conferences are organized by a host branch, with help from a faculty advisor and AIAA headquarters. Students prepare a paper on a subject of their choosing and submit it. The host school supplies a panel of aeronautical and astronautical professionals to judge the papers on their technical content. A panel of judges is also supplied to hear the papers at a presentation.

This allows students to get a real feel of presenting to their peers. Although not everyone in the aerospace industry presents papers at conferences, almost all go to conferences. The student conferences allow students to become comfortable in a conference atmosphere. Also, many professional aerospace people and AIAA members attend these conferences, so students are able to start networking before they ever leave college.

The winners of the regional conferences are supported to the AIAA Foundation National Student Conference held in conjunction with the AIAA annual Aerospace Sciences Meeting.

If writing a paper isn't what you would like to do to enhance your education, the AIAA Foundation also sponsors design competitions. These competitions allow you to design an actual product and get used to reading requests for proposals (RFPs) and preparing a proposal in response. The AIAA Foundation offers several different topics from which to choose. There are team graduate, team undergraduate, and individual competitions. These competitions not only allow you to understand and do actual design, but they have monetary value as well. First place receives $2,500, and a representative of the team is appointed to a technical conference to present the team's work. Second place receives $1,500, and third receives $1,000.

If you would like a little more hands-on type of work, the AIAA Foundation also sponsors a design/build/fly competition. In this competition, you and a team of students design a radio-controlled airplane to perform a specific function. The function could be to carry tennis balls in a certain pattern, fly a particular pattern with as many softballs or as much weight as possible, and so on. Your team writes a short report discussing the design process it went through to determine how and with what it would build its plane. Then, after the team has built the plane, it is brought to a central location (either Patuxent River, Maryland, or Wichita, Kansas) and flown against other planes in a "flyoff." The total score for each team is a combination of the report, design, and flyoff.

This event is very popular among the AIAA student membership. Usually more than twenty-five teams participate, including teams from outside the United States. Turkey and Italy often send teams to participate in the competition. In addition, many people come just to watch the competition. It isn't unusual to have 250 spectators at the three-day event.

OUTLOOK FOR THE FUTURE

Aerospace engineering is significantly impacted by government policies in the area of defense and space programs. While there is always a need for aerospace engineers, the availability of federal funding for research and development and production varies greatly. Therefore, the aerospace industry has a cyclical atmosphere, as many disciplines do.

As a result of the terrorist attacks on September 11, 2001, the aeronautical and astronautical community has experienced significant changes to vehicle technology. This has meant new opportunities in the industry. Therefore, the outlook for aerospace and aeronautical engineering is good through 2016.

EARNINGS

According to the U.S. Bureau of Labor Statistics (bls.gov), aerospace engineers had a median annual salary of $87,610 in 2006. This means that half of all mechanical engineers earned more than that amount and half earned less. The lowest 10 percent of mechanical engineers earned less than $59,610, and the highest 10 percent earned more than $124,550.

In 2007 PayScale.com reported that mechanical engineers with less than one year of experience earned a median salary of $56,255. Those with five to nine years of experience earned a median salary of $74,770. The median annual salaries reported in various employment sectors include:

Colleges and Universities	$70,590
Contractors	$60,602
Corporations	$74,883
Federal Government	$77,907
Nonprofit Organizations*	$85,074

*Aerospace Corporation is an example of a nonprofit employer of aerospace engineers.

ADDITIONAL SOURCES OF INFORMATION

Aerospace Industries Association (AIA)
1000 Wilson Blvd., Suite 1700
Arlington, VA 22209
aia-aerospace.org

American Astronomical Society (AAS)
2000 Florida Ave. NW, Suite 400
Washington, DC 20009
aas.org

American Institute of Aeronautics and Astronautics, Inc. (AIAA)
1801 Alexander Bell Dr., Suite 500
Reston, VA 20191
aiaa.org

Canadian Aeronautics and Space Institute (CASI)
350 Terry Fox Dr., Suite 104
Kanata, ONT K2K 2W5
Canada
casi.ca

International Astronautical Federation (IAF)
3/5 rue Mario Nikis
75015 Paris
France
iafastro.com

International Council of the Aeronautical Sciences (ICAS)
ICAS Secretariat
Anders Gustafsson
c/o FOI
SE–17290 Stockholm
Sweden
icas.org

NASA
nasa.gov
NASA's educational outreach is a good source of information. The NASA Why? Files (http://whyfiles.larc.nasa.gov/treehouse.html) is a website dedicated to students interested in aerospace.

Currently AIAA has an educational partnership with NASA and manages and organizes NASA's space station utilization conferences.

AIAA also has a contract with the Federal Aviation Administration (FAA) as a result of the September 11, 2001, attack. The FAA received thousands and thousands of e-mails, letters, and faxes about how to improve security. AIAA is working with the FAA to sort through and organize all of these ideas.

AIAA's booklet, *Careers in Aerospace Within Your Lifetime,* is aimed at eighth graders. It allows students to find out what they can do as an aerospace engineer and how to plan for it. It gives a general idea of what classes students need to take in high school and college to receive a degree in aerospace engineering. The booklet can be obtained by contacting AIAA Customer Service at custserv@aiaa.org.

14

AGRICULTURAL AND BIOLOGICAL ENGINEERING

Agriculture is central to a strong economy since a society must be able to feed its own people. In the United States, we are not only capable of feeding our own people but we have the capacity to feed people in other parts of the world. This capability is due in large part to the research and innovation of agricultural and biological engineers. Today, their work has grown in significance as new demands are placed on agriculture. For example, Americans are increasingly demanding more organically grown foods. We also look to agriculture for alternative fuels, such as ethanol. These demands mean that more effective and efficient ways of growing agricultural crops need to be developed.

In addition, global concern about the environment means we must find ecologically friendly ways of growing and harvesting crops. To ensure tomorrow's food production, agricultural and biological engineers constantly work to protect today's environment.

Agricultural and biological engineers make significant contributions to meeting the basic needs of society. These contributions include, but are not limited to, maintaining food quality, quantity, and safety; improving environmental quality; and enhancing the quantity and quality of our water resources.

Agricultural productivity is a key measure of an agricultural engineer's performance. As agricultural and biological engineers develop new tools, it becomes increasingly easier and more practical to produce, process, and distribute food and fibers.

The work of agricultural and biological engineers is increasingly important, as the food industry contributes $400 billion to the gross national product (GNP) of the United States and employs approximately twenty-five thousand engineers. Similarly, the construction industry uses more tonnage of wood, a biological material with unique properties, than all metals combined. In addition, more than 200 industrial products, not including pharmaceuticals, are produced with cell cultures that come from plants, animals, and microorganisms.

THE WORK THAT AGRICULTURAL AND BIOLOGICAL ENGINEERS DO

Agricultural and biological engineers utilize their knowledge of math, science, and engineering to address issues related to agriculture, food systems, natural resources, the environment, and related biological systems. Their skills are applied across the vast food-production chain, from the preservation of food products to the protection of natural resources. These resources include soil, water, air, energy, and engineering materials.

Some agricultural and biological engineers apply biotechnology, computer science, and knowledge-based programs to control equipment used in the production of food. For example, computerized systems such as the Global Positioning Systems (GPS) and the Geographic Information Systems (GIS) accurately guide the application of seeds, fertilizers, water, and chemicals by farm equipment that has onboard computers, laser sensing, and robotics. Other engineers are involved with environmental concerns such as air and water quality and soil erosion and loss. Still others develop renewable energy from sources that augment and conserve fossil fuels.

Today, agricultural engineering can be split into four major categories: bioprocess engineering, land and water resources engineering, bioenvironmental engineering, and off-road equipment engineering.

Bioprocess Engineering

Bioprocess engineering designs, develops, and manufactures value-added products through further processing of agricultural materials. Engineers work with the production of food, feed, pharmaceuticals, nutraceuticals, fuels, lubricants, polymers, and chemicals. They use biological, thermal, chemical, and mechanical processing to develop new products and to design processing systems. Those systems include, but are not limited to, process control development, bioreactor design, scale-up of processes, upstream and downstream processing, and organic waste utilization. Some of the specializations of bioprocess engineering are food process engineering, primary processing, bioprocessing, bioremediation, and timber engineering.

Food Process Engineering. Engineers in this area design the processes used to manufacture food products to ensure that our food is safe and of the highest quality.

Primary Processing. Engineers specializing in primary processing use knowledge of how biological materials are changed by natural enzymes and surface microorganisms so that raw materials can be harvested from land and water and stored to later become food stocks for a wide range of processing activities.

Bioprocessing. In bioprocessing the engineer designs products and then separates and purifies them through processes and control systems that implement cell-culture manufacturing, such as fermentation, which uses enzymes to accomplish various goals.

Bioremediation. In bioremediation the engineer designs and implements procedures that use carefully selected organisms (or genetically manipulated organisms) to break down toxic materials in order to restore the productivity of land and water.

Timber Engineering. Engineers in this area develop engineered wood products such as trusses, laminated beams, and wall panels.

Land and Water Resources Engineering

The purpose of land and water resources engineering is to manage production of biological materials while protecting the environment. Engineers who work in this area protect and preserve the environment through conservation of natural resources and pollution control. They apply biological, ecological, and engineering principles to develop production systems that conserve natural resources and minimize pollution through erosion control, groundwater and surface water quality management, storm water management, land development, and organic waste management. Some of the specializations of land and water resources engineering are erosion control, site development planning, water quality, waste management, bioenvironmental engineering, and off-road equipment engineering.

Erosion Control. Engineers in this area design terraces, meadow strips, and drainage systems to maintain productivity of agricultural land and improve water quality because runoff from agricultural land can erode topsoil and fill streams with sediment.

Site Development Planning. In this specialty, engineers recommend and/or implement needed controls for storm water runoff or to improve water quality in order to positively impact surrounding biological systems for agricultural production.

Water Quality. Engineers concerned with water quality analyze and design mechanisms by which water flow interacts with soil microorganisms and plants.

Waste Management. Engineers in this area devise methods to return waste from animal production facilities and water treatment plants to the land in a sustainable manner, improve the ability of crops to use nutrients, and avoid contamination of surface and groundwater.

Bioenvironmental Engineering

In bioenvironmental engineering, the engineer is concerned with the design and development of building layout, structural analysis, indoor air quality and ventilation, plumbing and electrical systems, structural foundations, the treatment and handling of waste products, and animal and plant responses to the environment.

Off-Road Equipment Engineering

Engineers in off-road equipment engineering take part in the design, development, and manufacture of machines, engines, and machine components. They also are concerned with machine element analysis and guidance and control of machines that move, till, or otherwise interact with soils.

The American Society for Agricultural and Biological Engineers (asabe .org) has identified eleven specialty areas in which agricultural and biological engineers work.

Aquacultural engineering
Biological engineering
Energy
Food and bioprocess
 engineering
Forest engineering
Information and electrical
 systems

Natural resources
Nursery and greenhouse
 engineering
Power systems and machinery
 design
Safety, health, and ergonomics
Structures and environment

WHERE AGRICULTURAL AND BIOLOGICAL ENGINEERS WORK

Agricultural and biological engineers are employed in many settings. Some of the settings include engineering and environmental consulting firms, where they validate processes used in food and drug industries, prepare land use plans and environmental impact assessments, or build agricultural waste-handling facilities and equipment.

Opportunities for agricultural and biological engineers also exist in government agencies at local, state, and federal levels. Some examples at the state and federal levels are the Department of Conservation and Recreation, Environmental Protection Agency, Natural Resources Conservation Services, Department of Agriculture, Army Corps of Engineers, Food and Drug Administration, and Geological Survey.

For those in the bioprocessing area of agricultural engineering, opportunities exist in the food, pharmaceutical, and biotech industries and with numerous other companies that manufacture bio-based industrial products. Some employers in this area include:

A. O. Smith Corp.

Andrews Environmental
    Engineering, Inc.

Archer Daniels Midland
    (ADM)

Cargill

Case Corp.

Caterpillar Tractor, Inc.

Chrysler Corp.

ConAgra Foods

Cummings Engine Co., Inc.

Deere and Co.

Del Monte Foods, Inc.

Dole Foods, Inc.

FMC Corp.

Ford Motor Co.

General Mills, Inc.

General Motors Corp.

Kraft Foods

Lockheed Martin

M & M Mars

Monsanto

Morton Buildings, Inc.

NASA

Paramount Citrus

Pioneer Seed

The Pillsbury Company

Quaker Oats Co.

Ralston Purina

Sunkist

Trane Corp.

U.S. Armed Forces

U.S. Bureau of Reclamation

EDUCATION AND OTHER QUALIFICATIONS

Agricultural and biological engineering can either be pursued as its own major at universities that offer degrees in agricultural engineering, or as a specialty in such majors as civil engineering, chemical engineering, bioengineering, or mechanical or electrical engineering. Agricultural and biological engineering degrees are now offered under names other than *agricultural engineering*. Some are called biological systems engineering, bioresource engineering, bioenvironmental engineering, forest engineering, or food process engineering.

Nonetheless, preparing to study any of the programs related to agricultural and biological engineering begins in junior high school. At this level, it is important to take the appropriate math and science courses that form the foundation for someone to take three years of high school science, including chemistry and physics, and four years of high school mathematics, including trigonometry and calculus.

While the course work required for a bachelor's degree in agricultural engineering varies slightly from school to school, most programs include course work in mechanization, soil and water resource management, food process engineering, industrial microbiology, or pest management. In addition, most agricultural engineers take courses in computer science and engineering design. These courses prepare them for the senior capstone course where students design, build, and test new agricultural processes, products, or systems.

Students interested in the medical or veterinary field can usually follow the general agricultural engineering curriculum and select additional biology and chemistry courses as electives to prepare for medical or veterinary school. Agricultural engineering careers in business, industry, and government require a minimum of a bachelor's degree in an engineering field related to agricultural engineering. Positions in teaching or research require additional college education at the master's and Ph.D. levels. Regardless of the work setting, agricultural engineers need to continually update their knowledge and skills through continuing education courses and/or advanced degrees in order to remain current in the field.

The American Society of Agricultural and Biological Engineers (ASABE) website, asabe.org, provides a complete list of colleges and universities offering programs related to agricultural engineering.

Special Programs to Explore Agricultural Engineering

The ASABE sponsors the following five student design competitions:

AGCO National Student Design Competition
Agricultural Robotics Student Design Competition
Environmental Design Student Competition—Fountain Wars
Environmental Design Student Competition—Open Format
1/4 Scale Tractor Student Design Competition

The goal of all competitions is to be educational and fun for students interested in pursuing careers in agricultural and biological engineering.

OUTLOOK FOR THE FUTURE

The ASABE sees a solid future for agricultural engineers. The society reports that there is a steady job market, competitive salaries, and interesting work that benefits society. In addition, according to the U.S. Bureau of Labor Statistics, the employment of agricultural engineers is expected to increase through 2016. In large part, this increase will be due to the retirement of a growing number of agricultural engineers. It will also be due to increased demand for more efficiently produced agricultural products, conservation of resources, and production of alternative fuels.

EARNINGS

In 2006, the U.S. Bureau of Labor Statistics reported that the median annual salary of agricultural engineers was $66,030. This means that half of the agricultural engineers earned more than $66,030 and half earned less. The lowest 10 percent earned less than $42,390, and the highest 10 percent earned more than $96,270.

PayScale.com reported that the median income for agricultural engineers, with less than one year of experience, was $34,803 in 2007. For agricultural engineers with five to nine years of experience, the median salary was $56,707.

ADDITIONAL INFORMATION

American Society of Agricultural and Biological Engineers (ASABE)
2950 Niles Road
St. Joseph, MI 49085
asabe.org

CHAPTER 15

AUTOMOTIVE ENGINEERING

The Society for Automotive Engineers asks, "What do satellites, micro-chips, and tires have in common?" The answer: They all converge when you get behind the wheel of today's new car. From message lights that tell you when the tires need to be changed to voice guidance systems give directions to your destination, automotive engineers are concerned about all of these "car-friendly" technologies because they drive consumer preferences. Automotive engineers are also concerned about "future-proofing" cars so that they don't become technologically obsolete as soon as they leave the showroom. Working with all types of industries, automotive engineers incorporate innovation and satisfy consumer demand.

THE WORK THAT AUTOMOTIVE ENGINEERS DO

Automotive engineering involves the design, development, testing, and manufacture of motorcycles, cars, buses, and trucks, as well as their sub-systems or components. It is a field wide open to the inquisitive engineer who wishes to be involved in a broad variety of disciplines and their applications.

Jobs in the field of automotive engineering include the application of mechanical engineering, chemical engineering, electrical engineering, materials engineering, aerospace engineering, computer engineering, and civil engineering. Additionally, automotive engineering makes use of virtually every other field of pure or applied science and technology.

The work of automotive engineers can be divided into three categories:

Product or design engineer
Development engineer
Manufacturing engineer

Each plays a distinct role. For example, product engineers design components or systems, such as brakes or electrical systems. Their work falls into thirteen sub-categories:

Assembly feasibility	Package/ergonomics
Climate control	engineering
Cost	Performance
Drivability	Program timing
Durability/corrosion	Safety engineering
engineering	Shift quality
Fuel economy/emissions	Vehicle dynamics
Noise, vibration, and harshness	
engineering	

The development engineer is responsible for making sure that all engineered components can be assembled in the car, bus, van, SUV, truck, or motorcycle and meet all of the requirements of the government, manufacturing facility, and customer. The development engineer sees the big picture when it comes to assembly of the vehicle. It is the job of the development engineer to test, validate, and certify the complete vehicle, not just each component.

It is the responsibility of the manufacturing engineer to plan and engineer the assembly of the whole vehicle. Interestingly, at Toyota, the career path of manufacturing engineers is considered more prestigious than that of design or development engineers! After all, these are the people who make sure you get the vehicle you are expecting.

Manufacturing engineers typically work with statistics and process controls. They also validate the processes that produce the parts that go into each vehicle. This assures that each part meets the quality standards of the company.

Product, development, and manufacturing engineers are not the only engineers involved in the field of automotive engineering. Other engineering expertise is also needed, including aerodynamics engineers, body engineers, quality engineers, and logistics/transportation engineers as well as environmental and biomedical engineers.

Overall, automotive engineers work to develop and enhance vehicle efficiency, performance, reliability, and safety. Their responsibilities can include:

- Analysis of vehicle structures, using finite element analysis methods
- Precision mechanical designs, using two-dimensional layout and detail drawings and computer-aided design (CAD) software, such as AutoCad or ProEngineering
- Failure analysis
- Testing of vehicle and engine electrical/electronic systems
- Development of new or modified component designs
- Creation of prototype design drawings (including 3-D and wire-frame drawings) using computer-aided three-dimensional interactive application (CATIA) software

WHERE AUTOMOTIVE ENGINEERS WORK

Automotive engineers are employed in the traditional automobile manufacturing industry at companies such as Ford Motor, General Motors, Chrysler, Toyota, Honda, BMW, Mitsubishi, and so on. However, many more automotive engineers are employed in automotive support services such as the electronic components industry, the tire industry, the fabricated plastics and metals industries, and the transportation industry. A partial list of suppliers to the automotive industry includes:

3M Corporation
A.J. Rose Manufacturing
Amoco
AC Delco
Advanced Cast Products
Advanced Composites Group,
    Inc.
ALCOA
Allied Tube
American Precision Casting
Anchor-Harvey Components,
    Inc.
Arco Chemicals Company
Armstrong Industrial
    Specialties, Inc.
Ashland Chemical Company
BASF
BASF Plastic Material Products
Bayer Corp.
BF Goodrich Company
Borg Indak, Inc.
BorgWarner Automotive
Breed Technologies
CADSI
Castrol
Caterpillar (engines)
Cherry Corp.
Cherry Semiconductor
Chicago Miniature Lamp, Inc.
Chicago Rawhide
Cooper Automotive
Cooper Tire and Rubber
    Company
Cummins Engine Company
Dana
Delco Electronics Corp.
Delphi Automotive Systems

Diamondback
Dow Automotive
Dow Chemical
Dunlop Tire Corp.
Dupont Automotive
Dura Automotive Systems, Inc.
Eaton
Federal Mogul
General Electric
Goodyear
Hewlett-Packard
Hitachi America Ltd.
Hitachi Automotive Products
    (USA)
Hitachi Automotive Products,
    Inc.
Honeywell, Inc.
Illinois Tool Work
Illinois Tool Works Fluid
    Products
ITT Automotive
Johnson Controls
LTV Corp.
Marmon Group–Automotive
Monsanto Co.
Morton International
Motorola, Inc.
National Steel
Navistar International
New Venture Gear, Inc.
Osram Sylvania
Owens-Corning
Panasonic Automotive
    Electronics Co.
Parker Hannifin
PPG Industries
Siemens Automotive

Tenneco
Texas Instruments
Textron
TRW, Inc.

USX Corp.
Valvoline
Visteon
Yokohama Tire Corp.

An emerging employment area for automotive engineers is in the motorsport industry. Competitive racing of motorcycles and automobiles has grown tremendously in the past few years, which has created new opportunities for automotive engineers. However, it is important to note that the field of motorsports is extremely competitive and fast-paced. Winning is everything, and if your team doesn't win, you can find yourself looking for new employment on short notice.

EDUCATION AND OTHER QUALIFICATIONS

Automotive engineering is one of those disciplines that must be pursued as a specialty area within mechanical, electrical, industrial, chemical, or materials science engineering. Similar to all other areas of engineering, automotive engineers should begin preparation as early as junior high school by taking as many math and science courses as possible. Although no four-year accredited colleges or universities award degrees in automotive engineering, many of the traditional areas of engineering (mechanical engineering, chemical engineering, electrical engineering, materials engineering, and aerospace engineering) provide related course offerings. Colleges and universities involved in automotive engineering will usually have active student chapters of the Society of Automotive Engineers (SAE).

There are more than 380 SAE chapters at universities worldwide. More than fifteen thousand student members participate in engineering projects, attend free section meetings, and benefit from free technical papers and publications. Many students build vehicles to compete in some of SAE's annual collegiate design competitions.

Special Programs for Automotive Engineering Students
The SAE offers competitions that challenge students' knowledge, creativity, and imagination. These competitions are Mini Baja, Aero Design, Formula

SAE, Supermileage, Walking Machine Challenge, and Clean Snowmobile Challenge.

• Mini Baja competition consists of three regional competitions where teams of engineering students design and build off-road vehicles that will survive the severe punishment of rough terrain and water.

• Aero Design competition provides an opportunity for teams of engineering students to conceive, design, fabricate, and test a radio-controlled aircraft that can take off and land while carrying the maximum cargo.

• Formula SAE competition provides an opportunity for teams of engineering students to design, fabricate, and compete with small formula-style race cars. The vehicles are judged in three categories: static inspection and engineering design, solo performance trails, and high-performance track endurance.

• Supermileage competition provides an opportunity for engineering students to design and build a one-person, fuel-efficient vehicle based on a small four-cycle engine. All vehicles are powered by a two-horsepower Briggs & Stratton engine in order to create a challenging engineering design test.

• The Walking Machine Challenge provides teams of engineering students an opportunity to gain design experience while building a machine with independent legs that walks, climbs, and maneuvers around objects.

• In the Clean Snowmobile Challenge, teams of engineering students are given the opportunity to redesign a snowmobile to improve its emissions and noise while maintaining its performance characteristics. Entries are judged on emissions, noise, fuel economy/range, acceleration, power, and design.

OUTLOOK FOR THE FUTURE

The outlook for automotive engineers is good. The number of people employed in this occupation is expected to remain stable or increase slightly during the next two to three years. With the pending retirement of baby boomers, more opportunities will be available for those who are prepared for and experienced in automotive engineering.

EARNINGS

According to a 2007 report from PayScale.com, the median salary for automotive engineers with less than one year of experience was $55,133. This means that half of these automotive engineers make more than $55,133 and half make less. For engineers with five to nine years of experience, the median salary was $66,378. The same report stated that the median salary for automotive engineers working for automotive companies and suppliers was $71,252, for private firms it was $59,700, and for race teams it was $56,218.

ADDITIONAL SOURCES OF INFORMATION

American Society of Body Engineers (ASBE)
P.O. Box 80363
Rochester, MI 48308
asbe.com

Society of Automotive Engineers, Inc. (SAE)
400 Commonwealth Dr.
Warrendale, PA 15096
sae.org

CHAPTER 16

BIOMEDICAL ENGINEERING

Professor Larry McIntire, Chairman of the Biomedical Engineering Department at Georgia Tech, says that we are at the beginning of the "Biomedical Century." That is because biomedical engineers are making rapid advances and producing important medical breakthroughs that are improving the quality of life. Biomedical engineers apply their knowledge of engineering and human anatomy to the discovery and maintenance of systems and equipment used to assist medical and other health-care professionals. The many contributions of biomedical engineers include the development of the following:

- Miniature devices to deliver medications or inhibit growth of life-threatening cells at precise, targeted locations in order to promote healing or inhibit disease formation and progression
- Artificial biomaterials to replace bones, cartilages, ligaments, tendons, and spinal discs
- Automated monitors used by doctors to monitor surgical and intensive care patients and to monitor the unborn fetus in pregnant women, and by astronauts in space and deep-sea divers to monitor bodily functions under unusual circumstances
- Artificial hearts and heart valves, joint replacements, hearing aids, cardiac pacemakers, artificial kidneys, blood oxygenators, synthetic blood vessels, and prosthetic devices such as artificial arms and legs

• Advanced therapeutic and surgical devices such as laser systems for eye surgery and automated delivery of insulin

• Customized software to control medical instruments and to conduct data acquisition and analysis

• Medical imaging systems (MRIs and ultrasound), which are noninvasive diagnostic procedures, making them less painful for patients

The Biomedical Engineering Society (BMES) lists nine facts about biomedical engineering. How many do you already know?

1. Biomedical engineers play a significant role in mapping the human genome, robotics, tissue engineering, and nanotechnology.

2. Biomedical engineering has the highest percentage of female students in all of the engineering specialties.

3. Many biomedical engineering graduates go on to medical school. The percentage of students applying to medical school is as high as 50 percent in some programs.

4. There are fifteen chapters of the national biomedical engineering honor society, Alpha Eta Mu Beta, located on college campuses throughout the United States.

5. BMES has more than eighty-seven student chapters on college and university campuses.

6. Judith A. Resnick, Ph.D., a U.S. astronaut who died when *Challenger* exploded in 1986, was a biomedical engineer working at the National Institutes of Health (NIH) from 1974 to 1977.

7. Willem Kolff, M.D., Ph.D., a biomedical engineer and physician, designed early artificial hearts and the first kidney-dialysis machine. He supervised the first implanted artificial heart into Barney Clark, and his latest work is on a portable artificial lung.

8. The NIH has a new institute for biomedical engineering and imaging. The institute coordinates with the biomedical imaging and bioengineering programs of other agencies and NIH institutes to support imaging and engineering research with potential medical applications and facilitates the transfer of such technologies to medical applications.

9. A single U.S. foundation, the Whitaker Foundation in Arlington, Virginia, has made significant contributions to the development of this profession. Whitaker Foundation grants more than doubled the number of

biomedical engineering academic programs in the United States by adding thirty-eight new departments in this field.

Source: http://www.bmes.org/careers.asp#difference_between

THE WORK THAT BIOMEDICAL ENGINEERS DO

Biomedical engineers use their knowledge of science and engineering to analyze and solve problems in biology and medicine. Their work provides continued advancement of the health-care system through the design and improvement of instruments, devices, and software. It is a field of continual change and rapid advancement of technology.

As with other engineers, biomedical engineers work in teams. However, their teams are made up of other health-care professionals, including physicians, nurses, therapists, and technicians. Some of the well-established specialty areas within the biomedical engineering field are:

Bioinstrumentation
Biomaterials
Biomechanics
Cellular, tissue, and genetic engineering
Clinical engineering
Medical imaging
Orthopedic bioengineering
Rehabilitation engineering
Systems physiology

Biomedical engineers usually function as part of a medical team and are often the only professional engineer on the team. In many cases biomedical engineers provide the technical interface between the manufacturer and the user of the medical equipment. Therefore, their interdisciplinary background and their engineering expertise is relied on heavily. Biomedical engineers assess requirements and then research, design, and fabricate electronic instruments, software applications, or mechanical devices to meet specific requirements. The role of the biomedical engineer is one of the most exciting and rewarding of engineering opportunities.

Bioinstrumentation Engineers. Bioinstrumentation engineers develop devices used to diagnose and treat disease. Computers are essential to bioinstrumentation, ranging from microprocessors in instruments performing small tasks to microcomputers that process large amounts of information in medical imaging.

Biomaterials Engineers. Biomaterials engineers research, identify, and develop properties and behavior of living tissue and artificial materials used in implant materials to assure that the materials are nontoxic, noncarcinogenic, chemically inert, stable, and mechanically strong enough for a lifetime of use. Certain metal alloys, ceramics, polymers, and composites have been used as implantable materials, and new materials will be developed in the future.

Biomechanics Engineers. Biomechanics engineers apply classical mechanics (statics, dynamics, fluids, solids, thermodynamics, and continuum mechanics) to the study of motion, material deformation, and flow of fluids within the body.

Cellular, Tissue, and Genetics Engineers. Cellular, tissue, and genetics engineers work at the microscopic level. They use their knowledge of anatomy, biochemistry, and mechanics of cellular and subcellular structures to understand disease and to intervene at specific sites.

Clinical Engineers. Clinical engineers purchase advanced medical instruments for hospital settings and work with physicians to adapt the instruments to meet the specific needs of physicians and the hospital. They also develop and maintain computer databases of medical instrumentation and equipment records.

Medical Imaging Engineers. Medical imaging engineers use knowledge of physical phenomena, such as sound, radiation, and magnetism, to design and develop equipment that generates images to be used for diagnostic purposes.

Orthopedic Bioengineers. Orthopedic bioengineers apply engineering and computational mechanics to understanding the functions of bones, joints, and muscles, and for the design of artificial joint replacements.

Rehabilitation Engineers. Rehabilitation engineers are involved in the design and development of prosthetics and other assistive devices that enhance sitting and positioning, mobility, and communication.

Systems Physiology Engineers. Systems physiology engineers use strategies, techniques, and tools to understand the function of living organisms ranging from bacteria to humans. Computer modeling is used in the analysis of experimental data and in formulating mathematical descriptions of physiological events.

WHERE BIOMEDICAL ENGINEERS WORK

Biomedical engineers are employed in universities, industry, hospitals, medical and educational research facilities, and government regulatory agencies. In 2006, the U.S. Bureau of Labor Statistics counted more than 14,000 biomedical engineering positions, with nearly 20 percent of those being in the manufacturing industry, primarily medical instrumentation and supplies. The roles the biomedical engineers play in industry can range from feasibility research to distribution. Figure 15.1 shows the range of industry opportunities for biomedical engineers.

In addition to the large proportion of biomedical engineers who go on to pursue medical degrees, a significant number of biomedical engineers are employed in hospitals. Not all biomedical engineers find themselves in clinical situations. For every engineer working in a hospital, there are probably five engaged in industry. These are the engineers who design and investigate new techniques and technology, taking a problem and turning it into an opportunity and then a solution.

These engineers can also be found in an academic or pure research setting, taking their in-depth knowledge of electronics and combining it with medicine to provide the means for even greater enrichment of human life.

Figure 15.1 Engineering Career Areas in Biomedical and Bioengineering								
Discovery Research	Feasibility Research	Preclinical Trials	Clinical Trials	Premarket Approval	Large-Scale Manufacturing	Marketing	Technical Sales	Distribution

EDUCATION AND OTHER QUALIFICATIONS

The recommended high school preparation for majoring in biomedical engineering is the same as that for any other engineering discipline, except that life science courses should also be included. Advanced placement (AP) courses in math and science are strongly suggested.

Biomedical engineering is an engineering field that can either be pursued as a specialty within an engineering discipline such as electrical, mechanical, computer, chemical, or materials science engineering, or it can be pursued as a major in its own right at those institutions that offer specific preparation in bioengineering or biomedical engineering. Therefore, at the college level, there are basically two types of biomedical curricula. The first leads to a bachelor's degree in biomedical engineering. The second leads to a bachelor's degree in a traditional engineering field, such as mechanical, electrical, or chemical engineering, where the student elects to take courses in a biomedical option. These courses supplement the regular engineering curriculum.

Biomedical engineers are educated not only in the traditional engineering areas, but also in the biological disciplines of anatomy, biophysics, pharmacology, physiology, neurophysiology, and organic and biological chemistry. A list of programs in biomedical engineering accredited by ABET, Inc., is available from abet.org.

Because industrial need for biomedical engineers is typically concentrated at the graduate level, a large percentage of biomedical engineers continue their studies beyond the undergraduate level. And, a high percentage of undergraduates go on to graduate or professional school immediately after graduation. The proportion of students enrolling in medical school is generally higher than the proportion entering industry or graduate programs in biomedical engineering.

OUTLOOK FOR THE FUTURE

The demand for engineers with backgrounds in biology and medicine is growing rapidly. As a result, the number of biomedical engineering jobs is expected to increase by more than 30 percent through 2016. This increase is higher than the rate of other engineering areas, according to the U.S. Department of Labor. The Whitaker Foundation's funding of more collegiate programs in biomedical engineering has resulted in an increased number of biomedical engineers to fill those positions.

The rise in biomedical engineering jobs is attributed to an aging population and increasing demand for improved medical devices and systems, particularly as a result of the injured service personnel returning from the wars in Iran and Afghanistan. Specific areas of growth are expected to be in computer-assisted surgery, cellular and tissue engineering, rehabilitation, and orthopedic engineering.

EARNINGS

The U.S. Bureau of Labor Statistics reported that the median income for biomedical engineers was $73,930 in 2006, with the lowest 10 percent earning less than $44,930 and the highest 10 percent earning more than $116,330. In 2007, PayScale.com reported a median salary $52,221 for biomedical engineers with less than one year of experience and $70,922 for those with five to nine years of experience.

For those biomedical engineers employed in different market sectors, regardless of the amount of experience they had, PayScale.com reported the following median salaries:

College/University	$50,839
Company	$63,369
Government–Federal	$61,007
Government–State and Local	$54,576
Hospital	$51,204
Nonprofit Organizations	$63,613
Private Practice/Firm	$72,177

ADDITIONAL SOURCES OF INFORMATION

American Medical Informatics Association (AMIA)
4915 St. Elmo Ave., Suite 401
Bethesda, MD 20814
amia.org

American Society for Healthcare Engineering (ASHE)
One North Franklin, 28th Floor
Chicago, IL 60606
ashe.org

Biomedical Engineering Society (BMES)
8401 Corporate Dr., Suite 140
Landover, MD 20785
bmes.org

CHAPTER 17

COMPUTER ENGINEERING

Computer engineering is one of the fastest growing engineering fields because computers increasingly are part of our everyday life. Even your toaster probably has microchips! Car engines, microwave ovens, video games, watches, cell phones, pagers, laptop computers, and household appliances rely on computers.

Thanks to computer engineering advances, it is possible to produce high-quality, high-tech products for everyday use as well as for complex scientific, medical, and military use. The computer industry has made a strong comeback from the dot-com bust of 2000.

Computer engineering crosses the boundaries of many engineering disciplines and depends on the talents and services of other engineers in developing and implementing computer systems. This is particularly true for specialized computer systems, such as those designed for agricultural, biomedical, chemical, transportation, or automotive purposes.

Today, computer engineering encompasses diverse technological areas, including analog and digital electronics, computer architecture, computer-aided design (CAD) and manufacturing of VLSI/ULSI, intelligent robotic systems, computer-based control systems, telecommunications and computer networking, wireless communications systems, signal and information processing and multimedia systems, solid state physics and devices, microelectromechanical systems (MEMS), electromagnetic and electromechanical systems, data storage systems, embedded systems, distributed computing, mobile computing, real-time software, digital signal processing, and optical data processing. The range of jobs and job settings in the field of computer engineering is wide, depending on which of these areas of expertise you develop.

THE WORK THAT COMPUTER ENGINEERS DO

The opportunities in computer engineering cross the dividing lines of other engineering disciplines because the production of computers requires collaboration by many engineering specialists. When compared to most other engineering groups, computer engineers tend to perform more of their work in teams. In this collaboration, it is computer engineers who analyze solutions and then design, develop, manufacture, install, and test computer equipment and software, utilizing advanced communications or multimedia equipment.

Within the field of computer engineering, there are three major types of engineers: computer hardware engineers, computer systems engineers (including both software and network engineers), and computer information science engineers.

Computer Hardware Engineers

Computer hardware engineers—or electronics engineers—research, design, develop, and test computer hardware. They also supervise the manufacture and installation of computer chips, circuit boards, computer systems, keyboards, modems, and printers.

Computer Systems Engineers

Computer systems engineers determine what the computer is to do and how it is to perform those tasks. This engineering category tends to be divided into two groups. The first group is software engineers. These engineers design and develop software systems that combine the particular characteristics of the computer hardware with its software applications (programs) and/or operating systems. Their work enables the computer chips to function in a unified manner to produce a desired result.

The second group is network engineers. These engineers install and manage computer hubs, switches, routers, and firewalls, as well as information technology (IT) server structures running products such as Netware, Windows NT, Linux, and UNIX. They assure that all systems are running smoothly, and they take care of problems and plan new IT projects.

Computer Information Science Engineers

Computer information science engineers determine the manner in which the computer can best serve the user. They design databases to store and retrieve even the most minute bits of information on a multitude of subjects. Computer information science engineers emphasize the arrangement of input and output data rather than the mechanics of computing.

According to the Institute of Electrical and Electronics Engineers (IEEE), some of the areas in which computer engineers work are:

• **Artificial Intelligence.** Developing computers that simulate human learning and reasoning ability.

• **Computer Design and Engineering.** Designing new computer circuits, microchips, and other electronic components.

• **Computer Architecture.** Designing new computer instruction sets and combining electronic or optical components to provide powerful but cost-effective computing.

• **Information Technology.** Developing and managing information systems that support a business or organization. "IT embodies the hardware, software, algorithms, databases, tactics, and man-machine interfaces used to create, capture, organize, modify, store, protect, access, and distribute information for ultimate use by people," according to the Task Force on Information Technology for Business Applications.

• **Software Engineering.** Developing methods for the production of software systems on time, within budget, and with few or no defects.

• **Computer Theory.** Investigating the fundamental theories of how computers solve problems, and applying the results to other areas of computer science.

• **Operating Systems and Networks.** Developing the basic software computers use to supervise themselves or to communicate with other computers.

• **Software Applications.** Applying computer science and technology to solving problems outside the computer field. For example, in education or medicine.

WHERE COMPUTER ENGINEERS WORK

Computer professionals work in almost every environment including academia, research, manufacturing, service, and government. However, computer hardware and computer systems engineers tend to work in different settings.

According to the U.S. Bureau of Labor Statistics, computer hardware engineers held about 79,000 jobs in 2006. About 41 percent were employed in computer and electronic product manufacturing and 19 percent were employed in computer systems design and related services. Many also are employed in the communications industries and engineering consulting firms. Some of the major employers of computer engineers include:

Advanced Micro Devices, Inc. (AMD)	IBM Almaden Research Center
	IBM T.J. Watson Research Center
Dell	Intel
DRS Technologies, Inc.	Texas Instruments
Hewlett Packard	

In 2006, the U.S. Bureau of Labor Statistics found that computer software engineers held about 857,000 jobs. These engineers are employed in the computer and data processing services industry, which develops and produces prepackaged software as well as provides programming, systems integration, and information retrieval, including online databases and Internet services on a contract basis.

In addition, all types of computer engineers work for government agencies, manufacturers of computers and related electronic equipment, colleges and universities, and a wide range of industries. Those who work in industry are employed in all types and sizes of organizations, from start-up companies to large, established corporations.

Although computer engineering is traditionally part of electrical and electronics engineering, it has begun to be recognized as a separate engineering entity. It can either be studied as a specialty area within electrical engineering or it can be pursued as a college major in its own right at institutions that offer a degree specifically in computer engineering.

Because computer engineering is usually considered a part of the electrical and electronics engineering field, computer engineers will take the same general core courses as electrical engineers. In the junior and senior years, however, the degree and amount of specialization will vary according to a student's chosen track.

The following curricula show the typical courses required for electrical and computer engineering and for computer science and engineering.

Electrical and Computer Engineering
Circuits and electronics and labs
Computer architecture and switching
Electromagnetic fields
Energy conversion
Introductory computing
Linear systems
Logic circuits and lab
Math
Mechanics and thermodynamics
Oral/written communications
Physics and chemistry
Social science/humanities

Computer Science and Engineering
Computer hardware and microcomputers
Computer science and engineering electives
Engineering
Introductory computing
Lab and design work
Math

Oral/written communications
Physics or chemistry
Social science/humanities
Software engineering

Computer science and engineering programs generally have fewer courses in physics or chemistry. Instead of mechanics, thermodynamics, and energy conversion courses, the curriculum contains more electives in numerical methods, database design, operating systems, and artificial intelligence.

Four-year undergraduate computing programs are accredited by either the Computing Sciences Accreditation Board (CSAB) or ABET, Inc.

OUTLOOK FOR THE FUTURE

Because computers are now used to control such diverse things as the space shuttle, medical devices, and household appliances, the demand for all types of computer engineers will not only continue, it is expected to increase. The greatest need will be for those involved in designing, developing, managing, upgrading, and customizing increasingly complex systems. In addition, computer engineers who specialize in embedded systems will find themselves in increasing demand.

Employment opportunities for computer engineers will not only exist in the computer and office equipment industry, but in industries that are increasingly relying on computer applications. These industries include the medical, automotive, security, and transportation industries. Consulting firms will also provide increased opportunities for computer engineers. While computer engineering is a relatively young field, vacancies will also result from the need to replace retired workers as well as those who change career fields or leave the labor force.

EARNINGS

In 2006, the U.S. Bureau of Labor Statistics reported that the median annual income for computer software engineers was $79,780. The lowest 10 percent earned less than $49,350, and the highest 10 percent earned more than $119,770. Median annual earnings in the industries employing the largest numbers of computer software engineers were:

Computer Systems Design	$78,850
Insurance Carriers	$74,230
Management, Scientific, and Technical Consulting	$78,850
Management of Companies	$78,580
Software Publishers	$84,560

Similarly, in 2006, the Bureau of Labor Statistics reported that the median annual income for computer hardware engineers was $88,470. The lowest 10 percent earned less than $53,910, and the highest 10 percent earned more than $135,260.

In 2007, PayScale.com reported the median salary for computer software engineers with less than one year of experience was $57,605, and for computer hardware engineers with the same level of experience, the median salary was $53,385. For computer software engineers with five to nine years of experience, the median salary was $75,480. For computer hardware engineers with five to nine years of experience, the median salary was $79,840.

ADDITIONAL SOURCES OF INFORMATION

AeA (formerly the American Electronics Association)
5201 Great America Parkway, #400
Santa Clara, CA 95054
aeanet.org

American Society for Information Science and Technology (ASIS&T)
1320 Fenwick Lane, Suite 510
Silver Spring, MD 20910
asis.org

Association for Computing Machinery (ACM)
2 Penn Plaza, Suite 701
New York, NY 10121
acm.org

Association for Women in Computing (AWC)
41 Sutter St., Suite 1006
San Francisco, CA 94104
awc-hq.org

Computer Science Accreditation Board, Inc. (CSAB)
184 North St.
Stamford, CT 06901
csab.org

Computing Accreditation Commission (CAC)
c/o ABET, Inc.
111 Market Place, Suite 1050
Baltimore, MD 21202
csab.org/acrsch.html
abet.org

IEEE Computer Society Offices
1828 L St. NW, Suite 1202
Washington, DC 20036
computer.org/contact.htm

Information Handling Services (IHS)
321 Inverness Dr. S.
Englewood, CO 80112
ihs.com

Robotic Industries Association (RIA)
900 Victors Way
P.O. Box 3724
Ann Arbor, MI 48106
roboticsonline.com

CHAPTER 18

ENVIRONMENTAL ENGINEERING

Environmentalist and former U.S. Vice President Al Gore called attention to the environment in a way that others have been unable to do. As a result, there is now a global concern that we must do something to clean up our environment or many species will be threatened with extinction. Today more scientists and engineers than ever before are placing a high priority on addressing the many environmental issues that we face.

Environmental engineering is leading the way. However, environmental engineering is not a new field. Its roots can be traced back to the 1800s and to the field of sanitation engineering. Today environmental engineers play a vital role in working to reduce the pollution and toxicants in our air, water, and ground in order to preserve a better quality of life for all living things. Environmental engineers have limitless opportunities in the type of work that they do.

THE WORK THAT ENVIRONMENTAL ENGINEERS DO

Environmental engineers use the principles of biology, chemistry, and engineering to develop methods of solving problems related to the environment. The American Academy of Environmental Engineers (AAEE) states that engineers in this field work in a wide variety of areas, and each area has a number of subcategories. The areas in which environmental engineers tend to work are:

Air pollution control	Recycling
Hazardous waste management	Solid waste disposal
Industrial hygiene	Storm water management
Land management	Toxic materials control
Public health	Wastewater management
Radiation protection	Water supply

According to the U.S. Department of Labor:

Environmental engineers conduct hazardous-waste management studies, evaluate the significance of the hazard, offer analysis on treatment and containment, and develop regulations to prevent mishaps. They design municipal sewage and industrial wastewater systems. They analyze scientific data, research controversial projects, and perform quality control checks. . . . They study and attempt to minimize the effects of acid rain, global warming, automobile emissions, and ozone depletion. They also are involved in the protection of wildlife. . . . They help clients comply with regulations and clean up hazardous sites, including brownfields, which are abandoned urban or industrial sites that may contain environmental hazards.

Environmental engineers work in many capacities. They are researchers, designers, planners, operators of pollution-control facilities, professors, government regulatory agency officials, and managers of programs.

WHERE ENVIRONMENTAL ENGINEERS WORK

In 2006, the U.S Bureau of Labor Statistics reported that environmental engineers held about fifty-four thousand jobs. These positions are divided fairly evenly among various manufacturing industries; federal, state, and local government agencies; and engineering and management consulting firms. Some employers of environmental engineers include:

Beta Corporation	GEI
CDM	Malcolm Pirnie
CH2M Hill	Metcalf & Eddy
ENSR	Montgomery Watson Harza
EQE	Tetra Tech

In the industrial sector, environmental engineers can work for chemical companies, pharmaceutical companies, pulp and paper mills, nuclear plants, and oil companies. In addition, environmental engineers are employed by universities and by research firms and testing laboratories.

There is a strong relationship between pollution and population. Many opportunities for environmental engineers exist in urban areas with large concentrations of people—both in the United States and around the world. Given growing populations, old style manufacturing and power generation systems as well as the increasing use of cars in other parts of the world, the need for environmental engineers is increasing internationally, particularly in Eastern Europe.

EDUCATION AND OTHER QUALIFICATIONS

It is possible to enter this field by studying a specialty area in chemical, mechanical, or civil engineering or by pursuing a degree in environmental engineering in its own right at institutions that offer more in-depth preparation in environmental engineering. Anyone interested in preparing for any one of these degrees should study algebra, geometry, calculus, trigonometry, physics, and chemistry in high school. However, for those interested in environmental engineering, it is also important that you take more high school biology. Advanced placement (AP) courses in math and the sciences is also strongly recommended.

The AAEE states that entry-level positions in environmental engineering require a B.S. in engineering. The degree can be in civil, chemical, mechanical, or environmental engineering. In addition to college courses in math, science, engineering mechanics, humanities, writing, and speaking, students interested in environmental engineering will take courses such as organic chemistry, computational modeling, fluid mechanics, hydraulic engineering, and engineering graphics. They may also take courses such as environmental engineering systems, environmental impact evaluation, public health engineering, community air pollution, sanitary engineering, ecosystems and ecotoxicology, aquatic chemistry, or environmental engineering design.

In the field of environmental engineering, a master's degree or a Ph.D. are strongly recommended. However, advanced degrees are no substitute for experience. Therefore, during the undergraduate program it is advisable to participate in cooperative engineering education (co-op), or at least summer internships. In some states, co-op experience may count toward the experience needed to sit for the second exam in the Professional Engineering (P.E.) license process.

OUTLOOK FOR THE FUTURE

According to both the AAEE and the National Science Foundation, there have never been enough environmental engineers. Now that worldwide environmental problems have grown more complex, the demand for environmental engineers continues to grow. In fact, through 2016, the U.S. Labor Department expects the employment of environmental engineers to increase.

Environmental engineers will not only be needed to meet new environmental regulations but to develop methods of cleaning up existing hazards. In recent years there has been a shift in the approach to environmental issues. Now the goal is to prevent environmental problems rather than trying to control or clean up problems that already exist. It is projected that this new emphasis will also increase the demand for environmental engineers.

Political factors impact the job outlook for environmental engineers more than most other engineering fields. When legislation reduces funding to enforce environmental regulations, job opportunities tend to decrease. Similarly, when funding is increased to enforce new or existing environmental regulations, opportunities increase. However, in recent years an unusual phenomena has occurred. While federal spending on environmental issues has decreased, state and local governments have become more aggressive in cleaning up the environment and taking significant steps to prevent environmental disasters. This means that more opportunities might exist on the state and local level than on the federal level. Compared to most other types of engineers, environmental engineers are more likely to be impacted by political factors and by significant economic downturns. During these downturns, there can be less emphasis on environmental protection issues. Therefore, it is important that environmental engineers stay abreast of political and economic issues as well as environmental issues.

In order to know where the environmental opportunities exist, it is important to be informed about federal, state, and local legislation and regulations that impact the field. Membership in professional associations can help keep you informed.

EARNINGS

In 2006, the U.S. Bureau of Labor Statistics reported that the median annual income of environmental engineers was $69,940, with the lowest 10 percent earning less than $43,180 and the highest 10 percent earning more than $106,230. The median salary for environmental engineers with less than one year of experience was $47,351, and for those with five to nine years of experience, the median salary was $62,383, according to Pay-Scale.com in 2007. Median environmental engineering salaries, by type of employer, included:

College and University	$52,397
Company	$59,166
Contract	$53,692
Government–Federal	$74,073
Government–State and Local	$55,909
Private Practice/Consulting Firms	$53,721

ADDITIONAL SOURCES OF INFORMATION

Air & Waste Management Association (AWMA)
One Gateway Center, Third Floor
Pittsburgh, PA 15222
awma.org

Alliance to Save Energy (ASE)
1850 M St. NW, Suite 600
Washington, DC 20036
ase.org

American Academy of Environmental Engineers (AAEE)
130 Holiday Court, Suite 100
Annapolis, MD 21401
aaee.net

American Council of Engineering Companies (ACEC)
Environmental Business Action Coalition (EBAC)
1015 Fifteenth St. NW
Washington, DC 20005
acec.org

American Industrial Hygiene Association (AIHA)
2700 Prosperity Ave., Suite 250
Fairfax, VA 22031
aiha.org

American Institute of Chemical Engineers (AICHE)
Three Park Ave.
New York, NY 10016
aiche.org

American Society of Civil Engineers (ASCE)
1801 Alexander Bell Dr.
Reston, VA 20191
asce.org

ASCE Institute (www.asce.org/instfound)
Environmental and Water Resources Institute (EWRI)

American Society of Mechanical Engineers (ASME)
Three Park Ave.
New York, NY 10016
asme.org

American Society of Safety Engineers (ASSE)
1800 East Oakton St.
Des Plaines, IL 60018
asse.org

American Society of Sanitary Engineering, Inc. (ASSE)
901 Canterbury, Suite A
Westlake, OH 44145
asse-plumbing.org

American Water Works Association (AWWA)
6666 West Quincy
Denver, CO 80235
awwa.org

Institute of Professional Environmental Practice (IPEP)
600 Forbes Ave.
339 Fisher Hall
Pittsburgh, PA 15282
ipep.org

National Council of Examiners for Engineering and Surveying (NCEES)
P.O. Box 1686
Clemson, SC 29633
ncees.org

National Council on Radiation Protection and Measurements (NCRP)
7910 Woodmont Ave., Suite 400
Bethesda, MD 20814
ncrp.com

Portland Cement Association (PCA)
5420 Old Orchard Rd.
Skokie, IL 60077
cement.org

Solid Waste Association of North America (SWANA)
1100 Wayne Ave.
Silver Spring, MD 20910
swana.org

Water Environment Federation (WEF)
601 Wythe St.
Alexandria, VA 22314
wef.org

MANUFACTURING ENGINEERING

Headlines might lead you to think that manufacturing is a declining employment sector. However, the Society of Manufacturing Engineers (SME) reports that "manufacturing is the largest single contributor to the wealth of the world's economies." If manufacturing has gone global, how will that impact your career as a manufacturing engineer? According to Steve Jahnke, Texas Instruments' Chief Architect, OMAP Symbian S60 and Linux SW Systems, the ability to work with both U.S. and offshore engineering and marketing teams is, and will continue to be, highly valued by manufacturers. This is one of the benefits of the "outsourcing" debate. He suggests that ten years ago, he might not have been as highly valued as he is now. His years of experience living and working in another country and his strong engineering knowledge have resulted in promotions and compensation comparable to M.B.A. consultants/finance specialists.

To assure the strength of the manufacturing sector in the United States, the federal government formed the Manufacturing Engineering Laboratory (MEL). The purpose of MEL is to contribute to improvements in the capabilities and performance of every phase of manufacturing. As a result of this commitment of research and funds, U.S. manufacturing has become very high tech.

Today's manufacturing facilities are no longer the old smokestack and dirt assembly line places that dominated the twentieth century. They now involve robotic devices, computer-integrated systems, e-commerce, green manufacturing, and other new technologies, making them dynamic and innovative places to work. A tour of a modern manufacturing facility is like a trip into a futuristic space and time. As a result, there is an increasing need for engineers who are trained for this work environment. It is not necessary to specifically major in manufacturing engineering to enter this field. Manufacturing engineers can pursue a specialty in such traditional majors as industrial, mechanical, electrical, or chemical engineering. However, in recent years more engineering schools have added manufacturing engineering as a major in its own right. This phenomenon reflects the increased demand by manufacturers for engineers who are highly educated in the field.

Manufacturing engineers not only like to make things, but they like to make them better, faster, and at a lower cost. They want to be involved from the initial design process to final production. These are the people who enjoy working with other people, as part of a team or as the team's leader.

THE WORK THAT MANUFACTURING ENGINEERS DO

Manufacturing engineers apply manufacturing sciences and technology to improve production. They utilize fundamental engineering skills based in mathematics, science, and the scientific method as well as contemporary tools and techniques to identify and solve manufacturing and service industry problems. They understand, analyze, and design industrial and service processes, systems, and work environments.

Manufacturing engineers deal with all aspects of the production process. They are the engineers concerned with the design and operation of integrated systems that produce high-quality, affordable products that utilize computer networks, robots, machine tools, and high-tech materials-handling equipment. In order to do so, manufacturing engineers take an interdisciplinary approach to their work.

Manufacturing engineers can specialize in a variety of specific technologies. One of the new and emerging technologies is "smart" materials. *Smart materials* include gels, ceramics, alloys, and polymers. For example, *smart gels* shrink or swell and can be programmed to absorb or release fluids. They can be used in agriculture, food, drug delivery, prostheses, cosmetics, and chemical processing applications. *Smart alloys* change shape in response to heat or cold. They can be used in couplers, thermostats, automobile, plane, and helicopter parts.

Other specialties include controlling chemical and other manufacturing processes, and expanding the use of microelectronics and manufacturing microsystems. In fact, some collegiate programs combine the study of manufacturing engineering with other technology areas so that graduates are prepared to work in specific manufacturing industries. An example of this type of program might be an aerospace manufacturing program that prepares students to work for manufacturers of small aircraft, jetliners, or spacecraft.

Manufacturing engineers assure that their solutions are economically viable and meet industrial health, safety, and all other relevant legislation. They are involved in the entire field of manufacturing engineering, including machine tools, materials processing, sensors and controllers, computer-integrated manufacturing and robotics, and manufacturing systems management and optimization. That is why SME has communities to which its members can belong. The association provides an around-the-clock live and online network to solve technical and business challenges facing manufacturing engineers. The network is comprised of the following eight key manufacturing disciplines.

Automated manufacturing and assembly
Forming and fabricating
Industrial laser
Machining and material removal
Manufacturing education and research
Plastics, composites, and coatings
Product and process design and management
Rapid technologies and additive manufacturing

The SME categories demonstrate the range of modern issues that face manufacturing industries. As a result, manufacturing engineers have responsibility for a wide variety of tasks, including such things as:

- Automating manufacturing facilities using computer-integrated technology
- Improving productivity by analyzing operations

- Developing scheduling systems
- Developing assignments for machines and equipment
- Implementing quality-control programs
- Identifying cost-effective material-handling and facility layout alternatives
- Designing management information systems
- Designing operator workstations—including seating, work surfaces, displays, and controls

WHERE MANUFACTURING ENGINEERS WORK

There is really no limit to where manufacturing engineers can work. Choices are not limited to certain industries as these engineers are needed wherever products are manufactured. They also are not limited by location because manufacturing is carried out around the world. In addition, manufacturing environments allow for a variety of experiences, which keep the work challenging and interesting. The U.S. Department of Labor's *Dictionary of Occupational Titles* provides a comprehensive breakdown of sixty-two businesses and industries in which manufacturing engineers are employed, ranging from abrasive and polishing industries to wood distillation industries and everything in between. In addition, service industries, such as health-care management and transportation, also provide opportunities for manufacturing engineers.

EDUCATION AND OTHER QUALIFICATIONS

Manufacturing engineering requires well-educated graduates because of the complexity of the work. To enroll in a collegiate manufacturing engineering curriculum, students should have at least two years of high school algebra and one year each of calculus, trigonometry, and physics. High school chemistry and calculus are also recommended.

The first two years of the college curriculum include fundamental courses in physics, chemistry, math, and engineering. Depending on the emphasis of the program at a particular college or university, courses in the last two years not only focus on advanced content in engineering and manufacturing but can include human-machine systems engineering, geographical information systems for engineering applications, advanced manufacturing processes, design for manufacture, electronic commerce, engineering products, engineering management, engineering data management, performance and quality improvement, and composite materials in mechanical systems. Other advanced courses include ISO 14000 international standards, microelectromechanical systems (MEMS), accident and liability risks, robust engineering, geometric tolerancing, project management, finance and accounting for project management, fundamentals of inventory management and control, and communications skills for managers.

Manufacturing engineering programs accredited by ABET, Inc., meet four primary criteria. They must demonstrate that graduates have proficiency in materials and manufacturing processes, and that they understand the following:

1. The behavior and properties of materials as they are altered and influenced by the manufacturing process
2. The design of products and the equipment, tooling, and environment necessary for manufacturing
3. The creation of competitive advantage through manufacturing planning, strategy, and control
4. The analysis, synthesis, and control of manufacturing operations using statistical and calculus based methods, simulation, and information technology

Most manufacturing engineering programs have a strong "practice-based" component. Some require structured internships, and others may take five years to complete because of the hands-on experience that students are required to obtain. Many manufacturing engineering programs either urge or require students to participate in cooperative engineering education (co-op). Gaining industrial experience to complement academic studies is highly regarded by those industries that seek graduating manufacturing engineers.

Once in the field, manufacturing engineers can obtain professional certification from SME in one of three categories:

- Certified Enterprise Integrator (C.E.I.)
- Certified Manufacturing Engineer (C.Mfg.E.)
- Certified Manufacturing Technologist (C.Mfg.T.)

Manufacturing engineers can also obtain a professional engineer (P.E.) license, which is highly recommended for those engineers working for companies with international facilities. After gaining several years of experience, many manufacturing engineers combine their technical expertise with their business experience to pursue an M.B.A.

OUTLOOK FOR THE FUTURE

According to WetFeet.com, manufacturing jobs have been moving overseas for a number of years. As a result, manufacturing is not considered to be a growth career field, despite specific growth spots, such as medical manufacturing and specialty electronics manufacturing. (wetfeet.com/Content/Careers/Manu facturing%20and%20Production.aspx). However, the global and decentralized nature of manufacturing today demands the special skills of manufacturing engineers, particularly if the engineer is multilingual. These engineers will be in demand to manage worldwide manufacturing operations.

EARNINGS

In 2007, PayScale.com reported that manufacturing engineers with less than one year experience had a median salary of $50,387. For those with five to nine years of experience, the median salary was $61,168. The median salary for various employer types is shown in the following table.

Company	$59,206
Contract	$61,175
Franchise	$61,120
Government–Federal	$61,460
Government–State and Local	$65,496
Private Practice/Consulting Firm	$56,834

It is important to keep in mind that the salaries for manufacturing engineers are most closely tied to the type of industry in which they work. For example, manufacturing engineers in the chemical industry should look at salary information for chemical engineers. Similarly, manufacturing engineers in the computer or aerospace industry will want to consider salary information for aerospace, electrical, or computer engineers. Otherwise it is recommended that the salaries of industrial or mechanical engineers be used as a guide.

ADDITIONAL SOURCES OF INFORMATION

American Architectural Manufacturers Association (AAMA)
1827 Walden Office Square, Suite 550
Schaumburg, IL 60173
aamanet.org

American Boiler Manufacturers Association (ABMA)
8221 Old Courthouse Rd., Suite 207
Vienna, VA 22182
abma.com

American Society of Mechanical Engineers (ASME)
Three Park Ave.
New York, NY 10016
asme.org

Association for Facilities Engineers (AFE)
12100 Sunset Hills Rd., Suite 130
Reston, VA 20190
afe.org

Institute of Electrical and Electronics Engineers, Inc. (IEEE)
Three Park Ave., 17th Floor
New York, NY 10016
ieee.org

IEEE Society Offices
IEEE Components, Packaging, and Manufacturing
Manufacturing Engineering Laboratory (MEL)
Technology Society

National Electrical Manufacturers Association (NEMA)
1300 N. Seventeenth St., Suite 1752
Rosslyn, VA 22209
nema.org

National Electrical Manufacturers Representatives Association
   (NEMRA)
660 White Plains Rd., Suite 600
Tarrytown, NY 10591
nemra.org

National Institute of Standards and Technology (NIST)
100 Bureau Dr., Stop 8200
Gaithersburg, MD 20899
mel.nist.gov

Society of Manufacturing Engineers (SME)
One SME Dr.
P.O. Box 930
Dearborn, MI 48121
sme.org

CHAPTER 20

PETROLEUM ENGINEERING

Contributed by John Fabijanic, California Polytechnic State University, San Luis Obispo

If you have not heard of petroleum engineering, you are not alone. According to Professor Craig Van Kirk of the Colorado School of Mines, many college graduates have never heard of petroleum engineering. However, it is petroleum engineers who search for oil and natural gas reserves and recover these natural resources for society's use.

With global demand for energy increasing 4 percent annually, the work in the oil and gas industry continues to expand. The scope is also expanding to address environmental concerns as well as the implementation of new technologies for more efficient and thorough retrieval of oil and natural gas. Some of those new technologies include high-directional angle drilling and reservoir management. The new drilling technique creates more flow from reserves and makes marginal reserves more profitable. Reservoir management uses mathematical modeling and 3-D seismic pictures to discover new reserves and to determine best locations for oil wells.

In the United States, oil and natural gas provide approximately three-fifths of our energy needs. Oil and natural gas fuel homes, workplaces, factories, and transportation and are the raw materials from which plastics, chemicals, medicines, fertilizers, and synthetic fibers are made. Formed by the decomposition of plants and animals under tremendous heat and pressure for millions of years deep underground, oil and natural gas are fundamental to modern society and will continue to be important well into the future even as efforts intensify to reduce dependence on fossil fuels.

THE WORK THAT PETROLEUM ENGINEERS DO

Petroleum engineers possess many skill sets and can take on many different responsibilities in the exploration for and retrieval of oil and natural gas. The overall responsibility of a petroleum engineer is to develop and implement the most cost-effective and efficient recovery of oil and natural gas. Petroleum engineers may specialize in a variety of areas, including, but not limited to, drilling engineers, production engineers, reservoir engineers, and environmental engineers. They may also be active in research and development.

Drilling Engineers. Drilling engineers design the drilling apparatus and support operations to extract fossil fuels. They work closely with geologists and other specialists to understand the geology and rock formations of the reservoir. These operations are often multimillion-dollar investments in time and resources.

Production Engineers. Production engineers develop processes to retrieve oil and natural gas in an efficient and cost-effective manner using techniques such as water, steam, gas, and chemical injection; computer-controlled drilling; and fracturing.

Reservoir Engineers. Reservoir engineers perform analyses to determine important parameters such as ideal recovery pressures. Reservoir engineers regularly use sophisticated computer models for simulating the petroleum reserve and the performance of different techniques of recovery. Much of the work involves the determination of cost-benefit analysis for the recovery effort justified for each petroleum discovery.

Environmental Engineers. Petroleum engineers specializing in environmental engineering are becoming increasingly important as environmental regulations and public demand for environmental protection become more prevalent. According to Dr. John Reis, author of *Environmental*

Control in Petroleum Engineering, "the activities of finding and producing petroleum . . . can impact the environment, and the greatest impact arises from the release of wastes into the environment in concentrations that are not naturally found."

Petroleum engineers develop solutions to environmental problems that occur during drilling and production processes. For example, if an offshore oilrig is going to be removed, petroleum engineers monitor the removal because it involves the use of explosives. A major environmental concern under these circumstances is the protection of endangered marine life in the area. Likewise, oil spills and accidents raise many environmental issues that must be addressed quickly and accurately. Petroleum engineers who have a complete knowledge of offshore oil and gas operations can work as interpreters of Federal, state and local environmental laws and regulations.

Research and Development. Only a small amount of the oil in a reservoir can be retrieved, even with modern techniques like water, steam, gas, and chemical injection; computer-controlled drilling; and fracturing to connect multiple reservoirs. Therefore, petroleum engineers are also involved in the research and development of new technology to more completely recover and lower the cost of retrieval of fossil fuels.

WHERE PETROLEUM ENGINEERS WORK

Petroleum engineers are found predominantly in oil and gas extraction, refining, and engineering and architectural services. Consulting firms and government agencies also employ petroleum engineers. In the United States the great majority of petroleum engineers work for larger companies that employ fifty or more workers. Some of those companies include:

BP	INTEC Engineering
Chevron	National Oilwell Varco
ExxonMobile	Petrobras America
Foster Wheeler	Shell
Fugro	Valero
Halliburton	Weatherford

While the preceding list represents large companies that employ petroleum engineers, it is important to know that the majority of companies that hire petroleum engineers are small. In fact, more than 70 percent of companies involved in the petroleum industry employ fewer than ten people. The greatest concentrations of opportunities for petroleum engineers in the United States are found in California, Louisiana, Oklahoma, and Texas.

Since the search for and retrieval of fossil fuels occurs worldwide, petroleum engineers can work in such exotic locations as remote jungles, deserts, mountain ranges, and offshore rigs. Those willing to work on assignment or be based overseas will find many opportunities in the petroleum industry.

For most petroleum engineers time at work is split between the office and field operations. The exact split of time is defined by the engineer's responsibilities and the scope of the project. Engineers working primarily at field locations often work nonstandard workweeks and hours, although the extra days or hours are generally well compensated. Positions consisting of primarily office-based work are not uncommon. Still other positions are on offshore rigs far from shore. In these locations, petroleum engineers may spend long periods at sea and live on a support ship.

EDUCATION AND OTHER QUALIFICATIONS

The Society of Petroleum Engineers advises those wanting to major in petroleum engineering to take courses in earth science, chemistry, physics, algebra, trigonometry, and calculus in high school. The petroleum industry is multinational in its scope, and the study of foreign languages is also recommended.

People who wish to enter the petroleum engineering field can either pursue a college degree in chemical, civil, environmental, mechanical, or electrical engineering, or they can pursue a degree in petroleum engineering in its own right at institutions that offer more in-depth preparation for the field. The college curriculum for a bachelor's degree begins with a focus on mastering the fundamentals of math, science, and engineering. Specialized courses leading to a petroleum engineering degree include courses in geology, formation evaluation, drilling, reservoir properties, and production.

A petroleum engineer will need a minimum of a bachelor's degree, although many companies prefer to hire candidates with a master's degree. Research positions often require a Ph.D.

OUTLOOK FOR THE FUTURE

According to the U.S. Bureau of Labor Statistics, employment of petroleum engineers is expected to increase through 2016, largely because there will be more jobs than qualified candidates since enrollment has been low in petroleum engineering and related majors. While most petroleum production areas in the United States have been explored, new technologies are making it possible to extract more oil and gas from these reserves. Additionally, more public lands have been opened up for exploration both on land and offshore. Worldwide demand for petroleum products is expected to continue to grow, and some within the industry see a significantly brighter future for the petroleum industry as it expands into the general and alternative energy markets and works to meet worldwide demand amid tougher and more stringent regulations. Therefore, the outlook for employment of petroleum engineering graduates is good.

Petroleum engineers work throughout the world, and those who are willing to work abroad and/or who speak one or more foreign languages will be in particular demand. Petroleum engineers trained in the United States are in demand with many foreign employers, and the best employment opportunities may be overseas, especially as the petroleum engineer gains more experience.

EARNINGS

The U.S. Bureau of Labor Statistics reported that the median income of petroleum engineers was $98,380 in 2006, with the lowest 10 percent earning $57,960 and the highest 10 percent earning more than $145,600. According to PayScale.com (2007), petroleum engineers with less than one year of experience had a median salary of $74,281 and petroleum engineers with five to nine years of experience had a median salary of $96,268.

ADDITIONAL SOURCES OF INFORMATION

American Institute of Chemical Engineers (AICHE)
Three Park Ave.
New York, NY 10016
aiche.org

American Petroleum Institute (API)
1220 L St. NW
Washington, DC 20005
api.org

Society of Petroleum Engineering (SPE)
P.O. Box 833836
Richardson, TX 75083
spe.org

CHAPTER 21

ENGINEERING TECHNOLOGY

Contributed by John Fabijanic, California Polytechnic State University, San Luis Obispo

Engineering technologists generally work in the applied part of the engineering spectrum and play an increasingly important role in our technological society. Specifically, engineering technologists solve practical industrial problems that impact the design and development of products such as autos, trains, aircraft, household appliances, and consumer electronics. While engineers simulate product behavior during manufacture or during use, it is the engineering technologists who make the products safer, more durable, lighter in weight, and less expensive to develop.

The activities of the engineering technologist usually include product development, construction supervision, technical sales, component design, field service engineering, and workforce coordination and supervision. Activities can also include manufacturing technology, which focuses on automated manufacturing and materials handling using computers to design and manufacture products or in process and quality control.

Engineering technology constitutes a wide range of skills and methods. Engineering technologists work closely with engineers. They assist engineers in planning and implementing designs and inventions. To understand what engineering technology is, let's take a closer look at the difference between the engineer and the engineering technologist.

In their jobs, engineers and engineering technologists often perform similar tasks; however, the engineer is more often concerned with developing the overall plans and designs, while the technologist is more concerned with the implementation or completion of a specific part of a plan or design. Put another way, the engineer is concerned with the application of scientific knowledge or "why" something is to be done. The engineering technologist is concerned with the actual performance and completion of the application developed by the engineer—the "what" needs to be done to achieve what the engineer has designed or specified.

As an example, a chemical engineer will know why two specific compounds when mixed will yield the desired results in a scientifically rigorous manner. The engineering technician will know what needs to be done to safely and efficiently produce and mix the compounds specified by the chemical engineer. The engineer's and technologist's areas of experience often overlap, and both are vital in the process of taking an abstract idea or goal to a successful reality.

The American Society for Engineering Education has defined engineering technology in the following way:

> Engineering technology is that part of the technological field which requires the application of scientific and engineering knowledge and methods combined with technical skills in support of engineering activities; it lies in the area between the craftsman and the engineer in the part closest to the engineer.

The technologist is concerned with achieving practical objectives through the application of procedures, methods, and techniques that have been proved by experience through the years. In developing plans and designs to solve complex problems, the engineer cannot develop a single, obvious best answer or plan. In solving technical problems that are sections or subsets of a large engineering plan or design, the technologist might be able to achieve a unique or specific solution.

The engineer must consider many nontechnical factors in developing plans and designs, including legal restraints, social impacts, economic factors, and aesthetic considerations. In solving technical problems, the technologist generally is not faced with such constraints and is usually able to concentrate on the physical and economic factors of the problem.

The engineer must exercise judgment in solving many problems to obtain the optimum benefit for society. In general, engineering technologists are not called upon to make such complex judgments, but they often must estimate and approximate conditions that cannot be completely known.

THE WORK THAT TECHNOLOGY SPECIALISTS DO

With the tremendous growth in technology and the increasing complexity of the applications of scientific and empirical technology, it has become more necessary for technologists to specialize in one of the many distinct branches of engineering and technology. At the same time, a separation has occurred in which certain people in a field concentrate on the development of designs and plans for the accomplishment of a given objective while another group of specialists concentrates on the practical application and implementation of those designs and plans. Hence, there is a need for both engineers and engineering technologists.

Finally, the individuals who are concerned with the practical applications—the technologists—have been divided into two classes, technicians and technologists. In general, these terms are used to designate persons with differing levels of education or experience in their field. The term *engineering technician* is applied to a person who has graduated from a two-year technology curriculum and has obtained an associate's degree in applied science or engineering technology. The term *technologist* usually is reserved for the graduate of a four-year bachelor of engineering technology program or for the technician who has gained wide experience in the field through many years of practice in engineering technology.

The field of engineering technology covers a broad spectrum of activities, and the engineering technologist specializes in one branch of engineering or another. There are four main branches of engineering technology:

- Civil engineering technology
- Mechanical engineering technology
- Electrical engineering technology
- Chemical engineering technology

Civil Engineering Technology

The most prominent activity in the civil engineering field is structural design. Technologists involved in this activity are concerned with some phase of the design of buildings, dams, and bridges. Structures must be designed and constructed to withstand their own weight as well as such natural forces as earthquakes and winds, and they must be suited to the environments in which they are built. The need to accommodate extremes in climatic and environmental conditions constantly presents new problems and challenges to the engineering team concerned with structural design and construction.

Civil engineering technologists often are employed directly in supervising and monitoring the construction of various facilities. In these activities, it is necessary to see that the structures under construction are built exactly according to the plans. Additionally, the technician and technologist often are charged with maintaining the quality of the construction materials. The engineering technologist working in construction also supervises the use of such heavy equipment as trucks, cranes, earthmovers, concrete mixing and placing equipment, and other machines.

Another key occupational area of the civil engineering technologist is the construction and operation of transportation facilities such as highways, airports, and railroads. The technologist can be involved in the initial planning phases for such facilities, assisting the engineer in predicting the growth of population, the volume of anticipated traffic, potential future problems, and possible alternate locations for transportation facilities. In these studies, the technologist will be called upon to give full attention to the environmental impact of the construction and operation of transportation facilities.

As in other fields where the construction of facilities is a necessary and important activity, in transportation engineering the technologist is involved in constructing facilities efficiently under varying conditions of terrain and climate. He or she is involved in surveying, mapping, and supervising construction. Finally, he or she also may be involved in the analysis of transportation systems to ensure the maximum efficiency of completed networks.

One of the oldest and most important areas of interest for civil engineers and technologists is that of hydraulics—the management of water resources. This area includes the collection, control, use, and conservation of water. Projects for flood control, drainage, reclamation, and irrigation are planned and designed by civil engineers and technologists who are specialists in hydraulics. They are also involved in navigation projects, water storage projects, and hydroelectric power plants.

One of the most important activities for civil engineering technologists specializing in hydraulics is assuring safe drinking water and effective sewage and wastewater disposal systems. With populations becoming more concentrated and modern industry growing rapidly, the amounts and kinds of pollutants poured into rivers and streams and other areas of the environment assure that engineers and technologists working in the area of water supply and wastewater treatment will find new challenges of ever-greater complexity.

In recent years, there has been a population shift from the country to the city. Civil engineering technologists working in construction, structural design, transportation, and water management are concentrating many of their activities in population centers, solving the problems caused by this redistribution of people. Some civil engineering technologists devote their time primarily to working with city planners and urban development agencies, assisting them in formulating plans for growth and the management of urban areas.

Mechanical Engineering Technology

As the name indicates, the mechanical engineering technologist quite often is concerned with the development of machines. Mechanical engineering technicians are found in the many steps in the process of taking an idea or goal and efficiently producing a useful end product.

In the initial research and development, mechanical engineering technicians will aid the design, manufacture, assembly, and testing of research equipment or prototypes. The technician may use machine tools such as lathes, mills, grinders, and shapers to produce components. Alternatively, the technician may do all of the drafting and commands on a computer that will then control a lathe or mill. As part of research and development, the mechanical engineering technician is often responsible for planning the layout of equipment, setting up test articles and test equipment, conducting tests, and writing reports.

As the project advances toward production, mechanical engineering technicians will, in addition to the duties performed during the prototype phase, be involved in production planning, determination of the assembly process, and establishment of machinery requirements for the parts to be manufactured in the most efficient and cost-effective manner possible. Some technicians will inspect the equipment, monitor the production process for problems, and suggest ways to improve the efficiency or reduce the occurrence of problems.

The mechanical engineering technician can perform some or all of these duties in as broad a range of endeavors as mechanical engineers are involved in. From the smallest plastic toy to the most complex nuclear power plant, all have mechanical engineering components that require mechanical engineering technicians to make things a reality. For example, mechanical engineers and technologists are deeply involved in the development of new power plants and mechanical configurations for automobiles and trucks. With the increasing scarcity of cheap petroleum fuels, emphasis is being given to developing more economical engines and power plants for vehicles. Mechanical engineering technologists assist in the design and perfection of automotive vehicles and supervise vehicle construction. Additionally, many technologists are employed in the search for ways to reduce air and noise pollution associated with automobiles and trucks.

Some mechanical engineering technologists are involved in developing other means of transport, including rapid transit systems and space exploration systems. Technologists can find employment with the manufacturers of aircraft and space vehicles, as well as with industries that produce such forms of transportation as elevators, conveyors, monorails, and escalators.

Mechanical engineering technologists are also concerned with the development and operation of heating and ventilating systems, including solar energy systems.

Electrical Engineering Technology

A student interested in electrical engineering technology might consider working in the field of electrical power generation and transmission, on the use of electrical power in the development of communications systems, or on developing new and more efficient lighting systems.

Electrical and electronics engineering technicians make up nearly half of all engineering technicians. With the continuing growth and importance of electronics to all fields of engineering, the need for electrical engineering technologists will also continue to expand. Electrical and electronics engineering technicians are involved in every phase of the design, testing, and manufacturing of electrical and electronic equipment. The range of projects can extend from communications, radar, data acquisition and measurement, medical monitoring equipment, and electronics control to computers.

The development of communications technology as a distinct area within electrical engineering technology has been very rapid during the last fifty years and continues at a great pace. Telecommunications is wide ranging; it makes possible everything from a traditional phone call to the entire array of modern multimedia and wireless communication. The sequence of communications devices based upon electricity and electronics began with the telegraph and has continued through the telephone, wireless set, radio, motion pictures with sound, telephoto transmitters, and television. A revolution in capabilities and availability of new technologies in communication and media has occurred in recent years, and these devices have been developed and manufactured in greater complexity with more reliability and at lower costs with each succeeding year. Now we have at our fingertips access to phenomenal technologies such as satellite communication and location, worldwide instant communication of many forms, and much more to come at an ever-increasing rate. Electrical engineering technologists can help develop and test new communication devices as well as supervise the manufacture of already developed devices.

Electrical engineers are instrumental in designing and maintaining electronics, computers, and electronic/computer-controlled systems. They design electronic data acquisition systems, electronic controls, and computer circuits; plan computer layouts; and formulate mathematical models of technical problems that can be solved by computers. These electrical and electronic systems can be for operating, controlling, and measuring the subject of the experiment or for controlling the processes of the manufacture of finished goods by controlling the machines making parts, mixing ingredients, and transporting goods.

Computers and electronic systems are found in every engineering field from testing through production and in every corner of the media and communications industry. The electrical engineering technologist is almost certain to become involved in some way in the design, manufacture, or use of such devices if this area interests him or her. Computers and electronics are integral parts of modern life, and there are any number of technologies on the horizon. Electrical and electronics technicians are required to design, test, and produce the current and future amazing array of electronic products for modern society.

Chemical Engineering Technology

Chemical engineering technologists prepare, separate, and analyze chemical substances. Relying heavily on a background in chemistry, they often study the composition and changes in composition of natural and synthetic substances. However, their activities are not limited to the preparation and analysis of chemical substances. The chemical engineer, as opposed to the chemist, is concerned with the maximum utilization of raw materials when mass-producing substances via technology that controls chemical and physical processes. Technologists work with chemical engineers in the development of new products, the design of new processes, and the planning and operation of chemical plants. They might assist chemical engineers in the manufacture and analysis of such chemicals as salts, acids, or alkalis, all of which are used in great quantities in modern manufacturing processes.

Technologists in chemical engineering also can be involved in the refining of such natural materials as petroleum and rubber. Petroleum is utilized as a fuel in such forms as natural gas, gasoline, kerosene, and fuel oil. The chemical engineering technologist can be involved in the refining and purifying of petroleum fuels as well as in the manufacture of chemicals from petroleum (petrochemicals). Chemical engineering technologists are being employed in ever-greater numbers in this growing field.

Another growing field in the chemical engineering industry is the synthesis of biochemicals, produced in nature by plants and animals. In this field, the chemical engineering technologist works on developing biochemicals in great quantity, at a reasonable cost, and with a high degree of purity. In other words, the technologist is employed in trying to reproduce, in full-scale manufacturing plants, the biochemical processes that occur in nature.

In all of the activities mentioned, the technologist is involved in the production of a given chemical substance through control of a chemical and physical process. Because of the importance of process control, many technologists also are employed in the study and perfection of basic chemical and physical processes. Within engineering plants, they assist in the control and perfection of chemical reactions. They are also concerned with the design of separation equipment and the development of control systems for the separation process.

One of the most important applications of separation combines the work of the chemical engineering technologist with that of the civil engineering technologist. These professionals collaborate in the use of separation operations to purify drinking water and to treat sewage waste. In utilizing such operations, chemical engineering technologists try to make reactions proceed as rapidly as possible with the lowest input of energy, to achieve the greatest efficiency and the lowest cost.

Some employers that hire engineering technologists include the following:

The Aerospace Corporation
Capital Group Companies
Cummins, Inc.
Dominion Energy (Dominion
   Virginia Power)
EMC Corp.
Harrison Steel Castings

Honda Manufacturing of
   Indiana
NVIDIA Corporation
Roche Diagnostics
Searle Exhibit Technologies
Sun Microsystems

EDUCATION AND OTHER QUALIFICATIONS

Within the last twenty years, a new engineering technology program leading to a bachelor of technology degree has been established in institutes, colleges, and universities throughout the United States. These programs developed for a number of reasons, the most important of which appears to be the increasing complexity of modern technology. The applications of science in today's world have become so varied and complex that it is now necessary to acquire a high degree of specialization. Thus, many two-year engineering technology programs have been expanded into four-year programs that compare in technical content to the four-year engineering programs that existed in this country a generation ago.

Students can earn a bachelor's degree in engineering or one in engineering technology. The engineering graduate very likely will hold a position in research, conceptual design, or systems engineering. The engineering technology graduate probably will be working in operations, product design, product development, or technical sales. The associate engineering technology graduate very likely will hold a position supporting an engineer's work.

A program leading to an engineering degree consists of courses in physical science, engineering science, and advanced mathematics through differential equations. The course of study leading to a bachelor's degree in engineering technology includes courses in technology, applied science, and mathematics through differential and integral calculus. The associate engineering technology program offers courses in science, skills, and mathematics through algebra.

Two-year engineering technician and four-year engineering technologist degrees are offered in several types of institutions, including the armed forces, technical institutes, community and junior colleges, and universities. Approximately 150 colleges offer programs leading to an associate's degree in engineering technology, and nearly 100 colleges and universities offer programs leading to the bachelor of engineering technology degree. The quality and content of training programs vary widely, and training programs should be investigated closely including researching the kinds of jobs graduates obtain, the facilities, and faculty qualifications. Additionally, it might be advisable to contact prospective employers regarding their preferences.

OUTLOOK FOR THE FUTURE

Employment opportunities for engineering technologists and technicians are subject to the same cyclical pressures as the engineers in each field. However, as technology advances and continues to expand its presence into all areas of society, the need for technicians and technologists to develop, run, and maintain this technology will also grow. The U.S. Bureau of Labor Statistics states that the overall employment of technicians and technologists is expected to expand as fast as the average for all occupations through 2010. As a result of the September 11, 2001, terrorist attacks on the United

States, it is likely that the new efforts at security both at home and abroad will rely heavily on expanded and new uses of technology, which should offer more job opportunities for technicians and technologists.

EARNINGS

According to the U.S. Bureau of Labor Statistics, the 2006 median annual earnings of engineering technicians, by specialty, were:

Aerospace Engineering and Operations Technicians	$53,300
Civil Engineering Technicians	$40,560
Electrical and Electronic Engineering Technicians	$50,660
Electro-Mechanical Technicians	$44,720
Environmental Engineering Technicians	$40,560
Industrial Engineering Technicians	$46,810
Mechanical Engineering Technicians	$45,850

The median annual salary for electrical and electronics engineering technicians was $50,660, with the lowest 10 percent earning less than $30,120 and the highest 10 percent earning more than $73,200.

Median annual salary in the industries employing the largest numbers of electrical and electronics engineering technicians are:

Employment Services	$38,910
Engineering Services	$48,330
Navigational, Measuring, Electromedical, and Control Instruments Manufacturing	$45,140
Semiconductor and Other Electronic Component Manufacturing	$45,720
Wired Telecommunications Carriers	$54,780

The median annual salary of civil engineering technicians was $40,560, with the lowest 10 percent earning less than $25,250 and the highest 10 percent earning more than $62,920. Median annual earnings in the industries employing the largest numbers of civil engineering technicians are:

Architectural Services	$42,310
Engineering Services	$41,180
Local Government	$45,800
State Government	$35,870
Testing Laboratories	$31,800

The median annual salary for aerospace engineering and operations technicians in the aerospace products and parts manufacturing industry was $52,060, and the median annual salary for environmental engineering technicians in the architectural, engineering, and related services industry was $38,060. The median annual salary for industrial engineering technicians in the aerospace product and parts manufacturing industry was $57,330. In the architectural, engineering, and related services industry, the median annual salary for mechanical engineering technicians was $43,920. Electro-mechanical technicians earned a median salary of $41,550 in the navigational, measuring, electromedical, and control instruments manufacturing industry.

ADDITIONAL SOURCES OF INFORMATION

A full package of guidance materials and information (product number SP-01) on a variety of engineering technician and technology careers can be purchased from the Junior Engineering Technical Society (JETS) at the following address. Free information is available on the JETS website.

Junior Engineering Technical Society (JETS)
1420 King St., Suite 405
Alexandria, VA 22314
jets.org

As a college student, you can join a number of social, honorary, and professional organizations affiliated with engineering technology. Once you are a practicing technologist, you can become certified. Practicing engineering technologists can join professional organizations such as:

American Society of Certified Engineering Technicians (ASCET)
P.O. Box 1536
Brandon, MS 39043
ascet.org

More information about engineering technician certification is provided by:

National Institute for Certification in Engineering Technologies
   (NICET)
1420 King St.
Alexandria, VA 22314
nicet.org

U.S. COLLEGES AND UNIVERSITIES OFFERING ABET-ACCREDITED ENGINEERING PROGRAMS

The following list of U.S. colleges and universities offering accredited engineering programs was provided by the American Society for Engineering Education (2008). All schools and programs accredited by ABET, Inc., are listed at its website, abet.org/accredited_programs.shtml.

Alaska

University of Alaska, Fairbanks
College of Science, Engineering & Mathematics
Fairbanks, AK

University of Alaska, Anchorage
School of Engineering
Anchorage, AK

Alabama

Alabama A&M University
School of Engineering & Technology
Normal, AL

Auburn University
College of Engineering
Auburn, AL

Tuskegee University
College of Engineering, Architecture & Physical Science
Tuskegee, AL

University of Alabama
College of Engineering
Tuscaloosa, AL

University of Alabama, Birmingham
School of Engineering
Birmingham, AL

University of Alabama, Huntsville
College of Engineering
Huntsville, AL

University of South Alabama
College of Engineering
Mobile, AL

Arkansas

Arkansas State University
Department of Engineering
State University, AR

Arkansas Tech University
School of Systems Science
Russellville, AR

Harding University
Searcy, AR

John Brown University
Siloam Springs, AR

University of Arkansas
College of Engineering
Fayetteville, AR

University of Arkansas, Little Rock
Donaghey College of Information Science & Systems
    Engineering
Little Rock, AR

Arizona

Arizona State University
Ira A. Fulton School of Engineering
Tempe, AZ

Embry-Riddle Aeronautical University, Prescott
College of Engineering
Prescott, AZ

Northern Arizona University
College of Engineering & Technology
Flagstaff, AZ

University of Arizona
College of Engineering and Mines
Tucson, AZ

California

California Institute of Technology
Division of Engineering and Applied Science
Pasadena, CA

California Maritime Academy
Vallejo, CA

California State Polytechnic University, Pomona
Pomona College of Engineering
Pomona, CA

California State Polytechnic University, San Luis Obispo
College of Engineering
San Luis Obispo, CA

California State University, Chico
College of Engineering, Computer Science & Technology
Chico, CA

California State University, East Bay
Hayward, CA

California State University, Fresno
School of Engineering
Fresno, CA

California State University, Fullerton
School of Engineering and Computer Science
Fullerton, CA

California State University, Long Beach
College of Engineering
Long Beach, CA

California State University, Los Angeles
College of Engineering, Computer Science & Technology
Los Angeles, CA

California State University, Northridge
College of Engineering & Computer Science
Northridge, CA

California State University, Sacramento
College of Engineering and Computer Science
Sacramento, CA

Harvey Mudd College
Department of Engineering
Claremont, CA

Humboldt State University
ERE Department
Arcata, CA

Loyola Marymount University
College of Science & Engineering
Los Angeles, CA

National Test Pilot School
Mojave, CA

Naval Postgraduate School
Monterey, CA

San Diego State University
College of Engineering
San Diego, CA

San Francisco State University
College of Science & Engineering
San Francisco, CA

San Jose State University
College of Engineering
San Jose, CA

Santa Clara University
School of Engineering
Santa Clara, CA

Stanford University
School of Engineering
Stanford, CA

University of California, Berkeley
College of Engineering
Berkeley, CA

University of California, Davis
College of Engineering
Davis, CA

University of California, Irvine
Henry Samueli School of Engineering
Irvine, CA

University of California, Los Angeles
Henry Samueli School of Engineering & Applied Sciences
Los Angeles, CA

University of California, Riverside
Bourns College of Engineering
Riverside, CA

University of California, San Diego
Jacobs School of Engineering
La Jolla, CA

University of California, Santa Barbara
College of Engineering
Santa Barbara, CA

University of California, Santa Cruz
Baskin School of Engineering
Santa Cruz, CA

University of the Pacific
School of Engineering
Stockton, CA

University of San Diego
Department of Engineering
San Diego, CA

University of Southern California
Viterbi School of Engineering
Los Angeles, CA

Colorado

Colorado School of Mines
College of Engineering
Golden, CO

Colorado State University
College of Engineering
Fort Collins, CO

Colorado State University, Pueblo
College of Education, Engineering, and Professional Studies
Pueblo, CO

Colorado Technical University
Colorado Springs, CO

Fort Lewis College
School of Natural & Behavioral Sciences
Durango, CO

United States Air Force Academy
Engineering Division
USAFA, CO

University of Colorado, Boulder
College of Engineering & Applied Science
Boulder, CO

University of Colorado, Colorado Springs
College of Engineering & Applied Science
Colorado Springs, CO

University of Colorado, Denver
College of Engineering & Applied Science
Denver, CO

University of Denver
School of Engineering & Computer Science
Denver, CO

Connecticut

Fairfield University
BEI School of Engineering
Fairfield, CT

Trinity College
Hartford, CT

United States Coast Guard Academy
Department of Engineering
New London, CT

University of Bridgeport
College of Science & Engineering
Bridgeport, CT

University of Connecticut
School of Engineering
Storrs, CT

University of Hartford
College of Engineering
West Hartford, CT

University of New Haven
School of Engineering
West Haven, CT

Yale University
Faculty of Engineering
New Haven, CT

District of Columbia

Catholic University of America
School of Engineering
Washington, DC

George Washington University
School of Engineering & Applied Sciences
Washington, DC

Howard University
School of Engineering
Washington, DC

University of the District of Columbia
School of Engineering and Applied Sciences
Washington, DC

Delaware

University of Delaware
College of Engineering
Newark, DE

Florida

Embry-Riddle Aeronautical University, Daytona Beach
College of Engineering & Aviation Science
Daytona Beach, FL

Florida A&M University/Florida State University
College of Engineering
Tallahassee, FL

Florida Atlantic University
College of Engineering
Boca Raton, FL

Florida Institute of Technology
College of Engineering
Melbourne, FL

Florida International University
College of Engineering and Design
Miami, FL

University of Central Florida
College of Engineering & Computer Science
Orlando, FL

University of Florida
College of Engineering
Gainesville, FL

University of Miami
College of Engineering
Coral Gables, FL

University of North Florida
College of Computing Sciences & Engineering
Jacksonville, FL

University of South Florida
College of Engineering
Tampa, FL

Georgia

Georgia Institute of Technology
College of Engineering
Atlanta, GA

Mercer University
School of Engineering
Macon, GA

University of Georgia
Biological & Agricultural Engineering Department
Athens, GA

Hawaii

University of Hawaii at Manoa
College of Engineering
Honolulu, HI

Iowa

Dordt College
Department of Engineering
Sioux Center, IA

Iowa State University
College of Engineering
Ames, IA

Saint Ambrose University
Davenport, IA

University of Iowa
College of Engineering
Iowa City, IA

Idaho

Boise State University
College of Engineering
Boise, ID

Brigham Young University, Idaho
College of Physical Science & Engineering
Rexburg, ID

Idaho State University
College of Engineering
Pocatello, ID

University of Idaho, Moscow
College of Engineering
Moscow, ID

Illinois

Bradley University
College of Engineering and Technology
Peoria, IL

Illinois Institute of Technology
Armour College of Engineering
Chicago, IL

Northern Illinois University
College of Engineering and Technology
Dekalb, IL

Northwestern University
McCormick School of Engineering
Evanston, IL

Olivet Nazarene University
Engineering Department
Bourbonnais, IL

Southern Illinois University, Carbondale
College of Engineering
Carbondale, IL

Southern Illinois University, Edwardsville
School of Engineering
Edwardsville, IL

University of Illinois, Chicago
College of Engineering
Chicago, IL

University of Illinois, Urbana-Champaign
College of Engineering
Urbana, IL

Indiana

Indiana Institute of Technology
College of Engineering & Science
Fort Wayne, IN

Indiana University-Purdue University, Fort Wayne
School of Engineering & Technology
Fort Wayne, IN

Indiana University-Purdue University, Indianapolis
School of Engineering & Technology
Indianapolis, IN

Purdue University, Calumet
School of Engineering, Mathematics & Science
Hammond, IN

Purdue University, West Lafayette
College of Engineering
West Lafayette, IN

Rose-Hulman Institute of Technology
Terre Haute, IN

Trine University
Allen School of Engineering & Technology
Angola, IN

University of Evansville
College of Engineering & Computer Science
Evansville, IN

University of Notre Dame
College of Engineering
Notre Dame, IN

University of Southern Indiana
Pott School of Science & Engineering
Evansville, IN

Valparaiso University
College of Engineering
Valparaiso, IN

Kansas

Kansas State University
College of Engineering
Manhattan, KS

University of Kansas
School of Engineering
Lawrence, KS

Wichita State University
College of Engineering
Wichita, KS

Kentucky

Murray State University
College of Science, Engineering & Technology
Murray, KY

University of Kentucky
College of Engineering
Lexington, KY

University of Louisville
J. B. Speed School of Engineering
Louisville, KY

Western Kentucky University
Ogden College of Science & Engineering
Bowling Green, KY

Louisiana

Louisiana State University
College of Engineering
Baton Rouge, LA

Louisiana Tech University
College of Engineering & Science
Ruston, LA

McNeese State University
College of Engineering & Technology
Lake Charles, LA

Southern University and A&M College
College of Engineering
Baton Rouge, LA

Tulane University
School of Science & Engineering
New Orleans, LA

University of Louisiana, Lafayette
College of Engineering
Lafayette, LA

University of New Orleans
College of Engineering
New Orleans, LA

Massachusetts

Boston University
College of Engineering
Boston, MA

Franklin W. Olin College of Engineering
Needham, MA

Harvard University
Division of Engineering & Applied Sciences
Cambridge, MA

Massachusetts Institute of Technology
School of Engineering
Cambridge, MA

Merrimack College
Department of Civil & Electrical Engineering
North Andover, MA

Northeastern University
College of Engineering
Boston, MA

Smith College
Northampton, MA

Suffolk University
Department of Engineering
Boston, MA

Tufts University
School of Engineering
Medford, MA

University of Massachusetts, Amherst
College of Engineering
Amherst, MA

University of Massachusetts, Dartmouth
College of Engineering
North Dartmouth, MA

University of Massachusetts, Lowell
Francis College of Engineering
Lowell, MA

Wentworth Institute of Technology
College of Engineering & Technology
Boston, MA

Western New England College
School of Engineering
Springfield, MA

Worcester Polytechnic Institute
Department of Engineering
Worcester, MA

Maryland
Capitol College
Laurel, MD

Johns Hopkins University
Whiting School of Engineering
Baltimore, MD

Loyola College in Maryland
Baltimore, MD

Morgan State University
College of Engineering
Baltimore, MD

United States Naval Academy
Division of Engineering & Weapons
Annapolis, MD

University of Maryland, Baltimore County
College of Engineering
Baltimore, MD

University of Maryland, College Park
The A. James Clark School of Engineering
College Park, MD

Maine

Maine Maritime Academy
Department of Engineering
Castine, ME

University of Maine
College of Engineering & Technology
Orono, ME

University of Southern Maine
Department of Engineering
Portland, ME

Michigan

Baker College
Engineering & Technology
Flint, MI

Calvin College
Engineering Department
Grand Rapids, MI

Ferris State University
College of Technology
Big Rapids, MI

Grand Valley State University
Padnos School of Engineering & Computing
Grand Rapids, MI

Hope College
Department of Physics & Engineering
Holland, MI

Kettering University
Flint, MI

Lake Superior State University
School of Engineering & Technology
Sault Ste. Marie, MI

Lawrence Technological University
College of Engineering
Southfield, MI

Michigan State University
College of Engineering
East Lansing, MI

Michigan Technological University
College of Engineering
Houghton, MI

Oakland University
School of Engineering and Computer Science
Rochester, MI

Saginaw Valley State University
College of Science, Engineering & Technology
University Center, MI

University of Detroit Mercy
College of Engineering & Science
Detroit, MI

University of Michigan
College of Engineering
Ann Arbor, MI

University of Michigan, Dearborn
College of Engineering & Computer Science
Dearborn, MI

Wayne State University
College of Engineering
Detroit, MI

Western Michigan University
College of Engineering and Applied Science
Kalamazoo, MI

Minnesota

Minnesota State University, Mankato
School of Science, Engineering, and Technology
Mankato, MN

Saint Cloud State University
College of Science & Engineering
St. Cloud, MN

University of Minnesota, Duluth
College of Science & Engineering
Duluth, MN

University of Minnesota, Twin Cities
Institute of Technology
Minneapolis, MN

University of Saint Thomas
Programs in Manufacturing Systems & Engineering
St. Paul, MN

Winona State University
College of Science & Engineering
Winona, MN

Missouri

Missouri University of Science & Technology
School of Engineering
Rolla, MO

Saint Louis University
Parks College of Engineering & Aviation
St. Louis, MO

Southeast Missouri State University
Department of Physics & Engineering Physics
Cape Girardeau, MO

University of Missouri, Columbia
College of Engineering
Columbia, MO

University of Missouri, Kansas City
School of Computing & Engineering
Kansas City, MO

University of Missouri, St. Louis
Joint Undergraduate Engineering Program
St. Louis, MO

Washington University
School of Engineering and Applied Science
St. Louis, MO

Mississippi

Jackson State University
School of Science & Technology
Jackson, MS

Mississippi State University
College of Engineering
Mississippi State, MS

University of Mississippi
School of Engineering
University, MS

Montana

Carroll College
Mathematics, Engineering & Computer Science
Helena, MT

Montana State University
College of Engineering
Bozeman, MT

Montana Tech of the University of Montana
Butte, MT

North Carolina

Duke University
Pratt School of Engineering
Durham, NC

North Carolina A&T State University
School of Engineering
Greensboro, NC

North Carolina State University
College of Engineering
Raleigh, NC

University of North Carolina, Charlotte
William State Lee College of Engineering
Charlotte, NC

North Dakota

North Dakota State University
College of Engineering and Architecture
Fargo, ND

University of North Dakota
School of Engineering and Mines
Grand Forks, ND

Nebraska

University of Nebraska, Lincoln
College of Engineering & Technology
Lincoln, NE

New Hampshire

Dartmouth College
Thayer School of Engineering
Hanover, NH

University of New Hampshire
College of Engineering and Physical Science
Durham, NH

New Jersey
College of New Jersey
School of Engineering
Trenton, NJ

Fairleigh Dickinson University
University College
Teaneck, NJ

Monmouth University
School of Science, Technology & Engineering
West Long Branch, NJ

New Jersey Institute of Technology
Newark College of Engineering
Newark, NJ

Princeton University
School for Engineering & Applied Science
Princeton, NJ

Rowan University
College of Engineering
Glassboro, NJ

Rutgers, The State University of New Jersey
College of Engineering
Piscataway, NJ

Stevens Institute of Technology
C.V. Schaefer, Jr. School of Engineering
Hoboken, NJ

New Mexico

New Mexico Institute of Mining & Technology
Socorro, NM

New Mexico State University
College of Engineering
Las Cruces, NM

University of New Mexico
College of Engineering
Albuquerque, NM

Nevada

University of Nevada, Las Vegas
Hughes College of Engineering
Las Vegas, NV

University of Nevada, Reno
College of Engineering
Reno, NV

New York

City College of the City University of New York
School of Engineering
New York, NY

Clarkson University
School of Engineering
Potsdam, NY

College of Staten Island, City University of N.Y.
Office of the Dean of Science and Technology
Staten Island, NY

Columbia University
School of Engineering & Applied Science
New York, NY

Cooper Union
Albert Nerken School of Engineering
New York, NY

Cornell University
College of Engineering
Ithaca, NY

✓ Hofstra University
Hempstead, NY

Manhattan College
School of Engineering
Riverdale, NY

✓ New York Institute of Technology
School of Engineering & Technology
Old Westbury, NY

New York State College of Ceramics at Alfred
School of Ceramic Engineering and Materials Science
Alfred, NY

Polytechnic University
Engineering Division
Brooklyn, NY

Rensselaer Polytechnic Institute
School of Engineering
Troy, NY

Rochester Institute of Technology
Kate Gleason College of Engineering
Rochester, NY

State University of New York, Binghamton
Watson School of Engineering
Binghamton, NY

State University of New York, Maritime College
Engineering Department
Bronx, NY

State University of New York, New Paltz
School of Science and Engineering
New Paltz, NY

State University of New York, Stony Brook
College of Engineering and Applied Science
Stony Brook, NY

State University of New York, Syracuse
College of Environmental Science
Division of Engineering
Syracuse, NY

Syracuse University
College of Engineering & Computer Science
Syracuse, NY

Union College
Engineering & Applied Science
Schenectady, NY

United States Merchant Marine Academy
Department of Engineering
Kings Point, NY

United States Military Academy
Office of the Dean of Engineering
West Point, NY

University at Buffalo, SUNY
School of Engineering & Applied Sciences
Buffalo, NY

University of Rochester
School of Engineering & Applied Sciences
Rochester, NY

Webb Institute
Glen Cove, NY

Ohio

Air Force Institute of Technology
Graduate School of Engineering & Management
Wright-Patterson AFB, OH

Case Western Reserve University
Case School of Engineering
Cleveland, OH

Cedarville University
Department of Engineering
Cedarville, OH

Central State University
College of Business & Industry
Wilberforce, OH

Cleveland State University
Fenn College of Engineering
Cleveland, OH

Marietta College
Marietta, OH

Miami University
School of Engineering & Applied Science
Oxford, OH

Ohio Northern University
T.J. Smull College of Engineering
Ada, OH

Ohio State University
College of Engineering
Columbus, OH

Ohio University
Russ College of Engineering and Technology
Athens, OH

University of Akron
College of Engineering
Akron, OH

University of Cincinnati/Engineering
College of Engineering
Cincinnati, OH

University of Dayton
School of Engineering
Dayton, OH

University of Toledo
College of Engineering
Toledo, OH

Wright State University
College of Engineering and Computer Science
Dayton, OH

Youngstown State University
Rayen School of Engineering
Youngstown, OH

Oklahoma

Oklahoma Christian University of Science and Arts
College of Professional Studies
Oklahoma City, OK

Oklahoma State University
College of Engineering Architecture & Technology
Stillwater, OK

Oral Roberts University
Department of Engineering
Tulsa, OK

University of Oklahoma
College of Engineering
Norman, OK

University of Tulsa
College of Engineering & Natural Science
Tulsa, OK

Oregon

George Fox University
Department of Engineering
Newberg, OR

Oregon Institute of Technology
School of Engineering, Technology & Management
Klamath Falls, OR

Oregon State University
College of Engineering
Corvallis, OR

Portland State University
Maseeh College of Engineering & Computer Science
Portland, OR

University of Portland
School of Engineering
Portland, OR

Pennsylvania

Bucknell University
College of Engineering
Lewisburg, PA

Carnegie Mellon University
Carnegie Institute of Technology
Pittsburgh, PA

Drexel University
College of Engineering
Philadelphia, PA

Gannon University
College of Science & Engineering
Erie, PA

Geneva College
Engineering Department
Beaver Falls, PA

Grove City College
School of Science & Engineering
Grove City, PA

Lafayette College
Engineering Division
Easton, PA

Lehigh University
Rossin College of Engineering & Applied Science
Bethlehem, PA

Messiah College
School of Mathematics, Engineering & Business
Grantham, PA

Pennsylvania State University, Erie
School of Engineering & Engineering Technology
Erie, PA

Pennsylvania State University, Harrisburg
School of Science, Engineering & Technology
Middletown, PA

Pennsylvania State University, University Park
College of Engineering
University Park, PA

Pennsylvania State University, Wilkes-Barre Campus
Lehman, PA

Philadelphia University
School of Textiles & Materials Technology
Philadelphia, PA

Robert Morris University
College of Engineering
Moon Township, PA

Swarthmore College
Department of Engineering
Swarthmore, PA

Temple University
College of Engineering Computer Science & Architecture
Philadelphia, PA

University of Pennsylvania
School of Engineering & Applied Science
Philadelphia, PA

University of Pittsburgh
School of Engineering
Pittsburgh, PA

Widener University
School of Engineering
Chester, PA

Wilkes University
College of Arts, Sciences & Professional Studies
Wilkes-Barre, PA

Villanova University
College of Engineering
Villanova, PA

York College of Pennsylvania
Department of Physical Sciences
York, PA

Puerto Rico

Polytechnic University of Puerto Rico
Dean College of Engineering
San Juan, PR

Universidad del Turabo
Jose Domingo Perez School of Engineering
Gurabo, PR

University of Puerto Rico, Mayaguez Campus
College of Engineering
Mayaguez, PR

Rhode Island

Brown University
Division of Engineering
Providence, RI

Roger Williams University
School of Engineering, Computing, and Construction Management
Bristol, RI

University of Rhode Island
College of Engineering
Kingston, RI

South Carolina

Clemson University
College of Engineering
Clemson, SC

The Citadel
School of Engineering
Charleston, SC

University of South Carolina
College of Engineering & Computing
Columbia, SC

South Dakota

South Dakota School of Mines and Technology
College of Materials Science & Engineering
Rapid City, SD

South Dakota State University
College of Engineering
Brookings, SD

Tennessee

Christian Brothers University
School of Engineering
Memphis, TN

Lipscomb University
Raymond B. Jones School of Engineering
Nashville, TN

Tennessee State University
School of Engineering and Technology
Nashville, TN

Tennessee Technological University
College of Engineering
Cookeville, TN

Union University
Department of Engineering
Jackson, TN

University of Memphis
Herff College of Engineering
Memphis, TN

University of Tennessee, Chattanooga
School of Engineering
Chattanooga, TN

University of Tennessee, Knoxville
College of Engineering
Knoxville, TN

University of Tennessee, Martin
School of Engineering Technology & Engineering
Martin, TN

University of Tennessee, Space Institute
Tullahoma, TN

Vanderbilt University
School of Engineering
Nashville, TN

Texas
Baylor University
School of Engineering & Computer Science
Waco, TX

Lamar University
College of Engineering
Beaumont, TX

LeTourneau University
School of Engineering & Engineering Technology
Longview, TX

Prairie View A&M University
College of Engineering & Architecture
Prairie View, TX

Rice University
George R. Brown School of Engineering
Houston, TX

Saint Mary's University–San Antonio
San Antonio, TX

Southern Methodist University
School of Engineering
Dallas, TX

Tarleton State University
Stephenville, TX

Texas A&M University, College Station
College of Engineering
College Station, TX

Texas A&M University, Commerce
College of Business & Technology
Commerce, TX

Texas A&M University, Galveston
Galveston, TX

Texas A&M University, Kingsville
College of Engineering
Kingsville, TX

Texas Christian University
Department of Engineering
Fort Worth, TX

Texas Tech University
College of Engineering
Lubbock, TX

Trinity University
Engineering Science Department
San Antonio, TX

University of Houston, Clear Lake
School of Science & Computer Engineering
Houston, TX

University of Houston
Cullen College of Engineering
Houston, TX

University of Texas, Arlington
College of Engineering
Arlington, TX

University of Texas, Austin
Cockrell School of Engineering
Austin, TX

University of Texas, Dallas
Erik Jonsson School of Engineering & Computer Science
Richardson, TX

University of Texas, El Paso
College of Engineering
El Paso, TX

University of Texas, Pan American
School of Engineering & Computer Science
Edinburg, TX

University of Texas, San Antonio
Division of Engineering
San Antonio, TX

University of Texas, Tyler
College of Engineering
Tyler, TX

West Texas A&M University
Canyon, TX

Utah

Brigham Young University
College of Engineering and Technology
Provo, UT

Southern Utah University
Computing, Integrated Engineering & Technology
Cedar City, UT

University of Utah
College of Engineering
Salt Lake City, UT

Utah State University
College of Engineering
Logan, UT

Virginia

Christopher Newport University
Newport News, VA

George Mason University
School of Information Technology & Engineering
Fairfax, VA

Hampton University
School of Engineering & Technology
Hampton, VA

Old Dominion University
College of Engineering & Technology
Norfolk, VA

Virginia Commonwealth University
School of Engineering
Richmond, VA

Virginia Military Institute
Engineering Division
Lexington, VA

Virginia Tech
College of Engineering
Blacksburg, VA

University of Virginia
School of Engineering and Applied Science
Charlottesville, VA

Vermont

Norwich University
Division of Engineering and Technology
Northfield, VT

University of Vermont
College of Engineering and Mathematics
Burlington, VT

Washington

Gonzaga University
School of Engineering
Spokane, WA

Henry Cogswell College
School of Engineering & Science
Everett, WA

Pacific Lutheran University
Tacoma, WA

Saint Martin's University
Lacey, WA

Seattle Pacific University
Division of Science & Engineering
Seattle, WA

Seattle University
School of Science and Engineering
Seattle, WA

Walla Walla College
School of Engineering
College Place, WA

Washington State University
College of Engineering and Architecture
Pullman, WA

University of Washington
College of Engineering
Seattle, WA

Wisconsin

Marquette University
College of Engineering
Milwaukee, WI

Milwaukee School of Engineering
School of Engineering
Milwaukee, WI

University of Wisconsin, Madison
College of Engineering
Madison, WI

University of Wisconsin, Milwaukee
College of Engineering & Applied Science
Milwaukee, WI

University of Wisconsin, Platteville
College of Engineering
Platteville, WI

University of Wisconsin, Stout
College of Technology, Engineering & Management
Menomonie, WI

West Virginia

West Virginia University Institute of Technology
L. C. Nelson College of Engineering
Montgomery, WV

West Virginia University
College of Engineering
Morgantown, WV

Wyoming

University of Wyoming
College of Engineering
Laramie, WY

APPENDIX

B

U.S. COLLEGES AND UNIVERSITIES OFFERING ABET-ACCREDITED ENGINEERING TECHNOLOGY PROGRAMS

The following list of U.S. colleges and universities offer accredited programs in engineering technology. This list was provided by the American Society for Engineering Education (2008). ABET, Inc., lists all ABET-accredited schools and programs at its website, abet.org/accredited_programs.shtml.

Alabama

Alabama A&M University
Normal, AL

Arizona

Arizona State University, Polytechnic Campus
College of Technology & Applied Sciences
Mesa, AZ

DeVry University, Phoenix
Electronics Engineering Technology
Phoenix, AZ

Arkansas

University of Arkansas, Little Rock
Donaghey College of Information Science & Systems Engineering
Little Rock, AR

California

California Maritime Academy
Vallejo, CA

California State Polytechnic University, Pomona
College of Engineering
Pomona, CA

California State University, Long Beach
College of Engineering
Long Beach, CA

California State University, Sacramento
College of Engineering and Computer Science
Sacramento, CA

DeVry University, Northern California
Fremont, CA

DeVry University, Pomona
Pomona, CA

Colorado

Colorado State University, Pueblo
College of Education, Engineering, and Professional Studies
Pueblo, CO

DeVry University, Westminster
Westminster, CO

Metropolitan State College of Denver
Denver, CO

Connecticut

Central Connecticut State University
New Britain, CT

Gateway Community-Technical College
North Haven, CT

Naugatuck Valley Community-Technical College
Waterbury, CT

Three Rivers Community-Technical College
Thames Valley Campus
Norwich, CT

University of Hartford
College of Engineering
West Hartford, CT

Delaware

Delaware Technical & Community College
Office of the President
Dover, DE

University of Delaware
Newark, DE

Florida

DeVry University, Orlando
Department of Electronics
Orlando, FL

DeVry University, South Florida
Miramar, FL

Embry-Riddle Aeronautical University, Daytona Beach
College of Engineering & Aviation Science
Daytona Beach, FL

Florida A&M University/Florida State University
Tallahassee, FL

University of Central Florida
Engineering Technology
Orlando, FL

Georgia

Augusta Technical College
Engineering Technology
Augusta, GA

Chattahoochee Technical Institute
Marietta, GA

DeKalb Technical Institute
Clarkston, GA

DeVry University, Decatur
Decatur, GA

Fort Valley State College
Agriculture, Home Economics & Allied Programs
Fort Valley, GA

Georgia Southern University
School of Technology
Statesboro, GA

Savannah State University
Savannah, GA

Savannah Technical College
Savannah, GA

Southern Polytechnic State University
School of Engineering Technology & Management
Marietta, GA

Idaho
Brigham Young University
College of Physical Science & Engineering
Rexburg, ID

Illinois
Bradley University
College of Engineering and Technology
Peoria, IL

DeVry University, Chicago
Chicago, IL

DeVry University, DuPage
Addison, IL

Morrison Institute of Technology
Morrison, IL

Northern Illinois University
College of Engineering and Technology
Dekalb, IL

Southern Illinois University, Carbondale
College of Engineering
Carbondale, IL

Indiana

Ball State University
Applied Sciences & Technology
Muncie, IN

Indiana University–Purdue University, Fort Wayne
School of Engineering & Technology
Fort Wayne, IN

Indiana University–Purdue University, Indianapolis
Indianapolis, IN

Purdue University (Statewide Technology)
College of Engineering or School of Technology
West Lafayette, IN

Purdue University, Calumet
School of Technology
Hammond, IN

Purdue University, Columbus
Columbus, IN

Purdue University, New Albany
West Lafayette, IN

Purdue University, North Central
Engineering Technology Department
Westville, IN

Kansas

Butler Community College
El Dorado, KS

Kansas State University, Salina
Salina, KS

Pittsburg State University
Department of Engineering Technology
Pittsburg, KS

Kentucky

Murray State University
College of Science, Engineering & Technology
Murray, KY

Northern Kentucky University
Highland Heights, KY

Louisiana

Delgado Community College
New Orleans, LA

Grambling State University
College of Science & Technology
Grambling, LA

Louisiana Tech University
College of Engineering & Science
Ruston, LA

McNeese State University
College of Engineering & Technology
Lake Charles, LA

Northwestern State University
Science & Technology
Natchitoches, LA

Southern University and A&M College
Baton Rouge, LA

Massachusetts

Benjamin Franklin Institute of Technology
Boston, MA

Northeastern University
College of Engineering
Boston, MA

University of Massachusetts, Lowell
College of Engineering
Lowell, MA

Wentworth Institute of Technology
College of Engineering & Technology
Boston, MA

Maryland

Capitol College
Laurel, MD

Prince George's Community College
Largo, MD

Maine

Central Maine Technical College
Auburn, ME

Maine Maritime Academy
Department of Engineering
Castine, ME

University of Maine
College of Engineering & Technology
Orono, ME

Michigan

Ferris State University
College of Technology
Big Rapids, MI

Lake Superior State University
School of Engineering & Technology
Sault Ste. Marie, MI

Michigan Technological University
School of Technology
Houghton, MI

Wayne State University
College of Engineering
Detroit, MI

Western Michigan University
Kalamazoo, MI

Minnesota

Minnesota State University, Mankato
School of Science, Engineering, and Technology
Mankato, MN

Missouri

DeVry University, Kansas City
Kansas City, MO

Linn State Technical College
Linn, MO

Missouri Southern State College
Joplin, MO

Missouri Western State University
Engineering Technology
St. Joseph, MO

Saint Louis Community College–Florissant Valley
St. Louis, MO

Southeast Missouri State University
Cape Girardeau, MO

Mississippi

University of Southern Mississippi
School of Engineering Technology
Hattiesburg, MS

Montana

Montana State University
College of Engineering
Bozeman, MT

Montana State University, Northern
Havre, MT

North Carolina

Central Piedmont Community College
Charlotte, NC

Fayetteville Technical Community College
Fayetteville, NC

Forsyth Technical Community College
Engineering Technology
Winston-Salem, NC

Gaston College
Dallas, NC

University of North Carolina, Charlotte
Charlotte, NC

Wake Technical Community College
Raleigh, NC

Western Carolina University
Kimmel School of CM & Technology
Cullowhee, NC

New Hampshire

New Hampshire Community Technical College, Nashua
Nashua, NH

New Hampshire Technical Institute
Concord, NH

University of New Hampshire
Durham, NH

New Jersey

Burlington County College
Pemberton, NJ

County College of Morris
Randolph Township, NJ

DeVry University, North Brunswick
North Brunswick, NJ

Essex County College
Newark, NJ

Fairleigh Dickinson University
Teaneck, NJ

Hudson County Community College
Engineering Technology
Jersey City, NJ

Middlesex County College
Edison, NJ

New Jersey Institute of Technology
Newark College of Engineering
Newark, NJ

Passaic County Community College
Paterson, NJ

New Mexico
Central New Mexico Community College
Albuquerque, NM

New Mexico State University
Las Cruces, NM

San Juan College
Farmington, NM

Nevada
College of Southern Nevada
Henderson, NV

New York
Alfred State College
Alfred, NY

Broome Community College
Applied Sciences Division
Binghamton, NY

Buffalo State College
Buffalo, NY

City University of New York, Bronx Community
Bronx, NY

DeVry University, Long Island City
Long Island City, NY

Erie Community College, North Campus
Williamsville, NY

Excelsior College, the University of the State of New York
Albany, NY

Hudson Valley Community College
Troy, NY

Mohawk Valley Community College
Utica, NY

Monroe Community College
President's Office
Rochester, NY

Nassau Community College
Garden City, NY

New York City College of Technology
School of Technology & Design
Brooklyn, NY

New York Institute of Technology
School of Engineering & Technology
Old Westbury, NY

Onondaga Community College
Syracuse, NY

Paul Smith's College
Paul Smiths, NY

Queensborough Community College
Bayside, NY

Rochester Institute of Technology
College of Applied Science & Technology
Rochester, NY

State University of New York, Canton
Canton, NY

State University of New York, Farmingdale
School of Engineering Technologies
Farmingdale, NY

State University of New York, Institute of Technology
School of Information Systems and Engineering Technology
Utica, NY

State University of New York, Morrisville
School of Science & Technology
Morrisville, NY

Technical Career Institutes
New York, NY

Vaughn College of Aeronautics & Technology
Academic Affairs
Flushing, NY

Ohio

Cincinnati State Technical and Community College
Cincinnati, OH

Cleveland State University
Fenn College of Engineering
Cleveland, OH

Columbus State Community College
Columbus, OH

Cuyahoga Community College, Metropolitan
Cleveland, OH

DeVry University, Columbus
Columbus, OH

Hocking Technical College
Nelsonville, OH

James A. Rhodes State College
Lima, OH

Kent State University, Tuscarawas Campus
Engineering Technologies
Kent, OH

Lakeland Community College
Engineering Technology
Kirtland, OH

Miami University
School of Engineering & Applied Science
Oxford, OH

Owens Community College
Engineering Technology
Toledo, OH

Sinclair Community College
Dayton, OH

Stark State College of Technology
Engineering Technology Division
Canton, OH

University of Akron
Community & Technical College
Akron, OH

University of Cincinnati
College of Applied Science
Cincinnati, OH

University of Dayton
Engineering Technology
Dayton, OH

University of Toledo
College of Engineering
Toledo, OH

Youngstown State University
Youngstown, OH

Zane State College
Zanesville, OH

Oklahoma

Oklahoma State University
College of Engineering, Architecture & Technology
Stillwater, OK

Southwestern Oklahoma State University
Technology Department
Weatherford, OK

Oregon

Oregon Institute of Technology
School of Engineering, Technology & Management
Klamath Falls, OR

Pennsylvania

California University of Pennsylvania
Applied Engineering & Technology
California, PA

DeVry University, Fort Washington
Fort Washington, PA

Pennsylvania College of Technology
School of Industrial and Engineering Technologies
Williamsport, PA

Pennsylvania State College, Altoona Campus
Altoona, PA

Pennsylvania State University, Worthington-Scranton
Dunmore, PA

Pennsylvania State University, Beaver Campus
Monaca, PA

Pennsylvania State University, Berks Campus
Reading, PA

Pennsylvania State University, DuBois Campus
Dubois, PA

Pennsylvania State University, Erie
School of Engineering & Engineering Technology
Erie, PA

Pennsylvania State University, Fayette Campus
Uniontown, PA

Pennsylvania State University, Harrisburg
School of Science, Engineering & Technology
Middletown, PA

Pennsylvania State University, Hazleton Campus
Hazleton, PA

Pennsylvania State University, New Kensington
New Kensington, PA

Pennsylvania State University, Schuylkill Campus
Information Sciences & Technology
Schuylkill Haven, PA

Pennsylvania State University, Shenango Campus
Sharon, PA

Pennsylvania State University, University Park
College of Engineering
University Park, PA

Pennsylvania State University, Wilkes-Barre Campus
Lehman, PA

Pennsylvania State University, York Campus
York, PA

Point Park College
Department of Natural Sciences
Pittsburgh, PA

Temple University
College of Engineering, Computer Science & Architecture
Philadelphia, PA

University of Pittsburgh, Johnstown
Engineering Technology Division
Johnstown, PA

Rhode Island
New England Institute of Technology
Warwick, RI

South Carolina
Aiken Technical College
Aiken, SC

Central Carolina Technical College
Sumter, SC

Denmark Technical College
Denmark, SC

Florence-Darlington Technical College
Florence, SC

Greenville Technical College
Greenville, SC

Horry-Georgetown Technical College
Conway, SC

Midlands Technical College
Columbia, SC

Orangeburg-Calhoun Technical College
Electronics Engineering Technology Department
Orangeburg, SC

Piedmont Technical College
Greenwood, SC

South Carolina State University
School of Engineering Technology and Sciences
Orangeburg, SC

Spartanburg Technical College
Spartanburg, SC

Tri-County Technical College
Industrial & Engineering Technology
Pendleton, SC

Trident Technical College
Charleston, SC

York Technical College
Engineering Technology
Rock Hill, SC

South Dakota
South Dakota State University
Brookings, SD

Tennessee
Chattanooga State Technical Community College
Chattanooga, TN

East Tennessee State University
School of Applied Science & Technology
Johnson City, TN

Middle Tennessee State University
Engineering Technology & Industrial Studies
Murfreesboro, TN

Nashville State Technical Institute
Nashville, TN

Pellissippi State Technical Community College
Applied Sciences/Technology
Knoxville, TN

Southwest Tennessee Community College
Memphis, TN

University of Memphis
Memphis, TN

Texas

Amarillo College
Amarillo, TX

Devry University, Houston
Houston, TX

DeVry University, Irving
Electronics Engineering Technology
Irving, TX

Houston Community College, Technology Center
Houston, TX

LeTourneau University
Division of Engineering
Longview, TX

Midwestern State University
Manufacturing Engineering Technology
Witchita Falls, TX

Prairie View A&M University
Prairie View, TX

Texas A&M University
College of Engineering
College Station, TX

Texas A&M University, Corpus Christi
Corpus Christi, TX

Texas Southern University
College of Science Technology
Houston, TX

Texas Tech University
College of Engineering
Lubbock, TX

University of Houston
College of Technology
Houston, TX

University of Houston, Downtown
Engineering Technology Department
Houston, TX

University of North Texas
Denton, TX

Utah
Brigham Young University
College of Engineering and Technology
Provo, UT

Utah Valley State College
School of Computing, Engineering & Technology
Orem, UT

Weber State University
College of Applied Science & Technology
Ogden, UT

Virginia

DeVry University, Arlington
Arlington, VA

Old Dominion University
College of Engineering & Technology
Norfolk, VA

Virginia State University
Petersburg, VA

Vermont

Vermont Technical College
Randolph Center, VT

Washington

Central Washington University
Industrial & Engineering Technology
Ellensburg, WA

DeVry University, Federal Way
Federal Way, WA

Eastern Washington University
Cheney, WA

Walla Walla Community College
Walla Walla, WA

Western Washington University
Engineering Technology Department
MS 9086
Bellingham, WA

West Virginia
Bluefield State College
Bluefield, WV

Fairmont State College
Fairmont, WV

West Virginia State College
Institute, WV

West Virginia University Institute of Technology
Montgomery, WV

Wisconsin
Milwaukee School of Engineering
Milwaukee, WI

SCHOLARSHIPS

The following organizations offer information on engineering scholarships, minority engineering scholarships, or other miscellaneous scholarships that may apply to engineering students. At the end of this appendix is a list of free online scholarship search services.

ENGINEERING SCHOLARSHIPS

The American Ceramic Society (ACerS)
www.acers.org/membership/levels/studentopportunities.asp

American Chemical Society (ACS)
acs.org (Type "scholarships" in the search box.)
   ACS offers Project SEED Scholarships and Minority Scholarships.

American Concrete Institute (ACI)
concrete.org/STUDENTS/ST_SCHOLARSHIPS.HTM

American Congress of Surveying and Mapping (ACSM)
acsm.net/scholar.html

American Council of Independent Laboratories (ACIL)
http://acil.org/displaycommon.cfm?an=13

American Geological Institute (AGI)
www.agiweb.org/mpp/index.html

American Institute of Aeronautics and Astronautics (AIAA)
aiaa.org/content.cfm?pageid=211

American Institute of Chemical Engineers (AIChE)
aiche.org/Students/Scholarships/index.aspx

American Institute of Physics (AIP)
aip.org/education/sps/programs/scholarships

American Nuclear Society (ANS)
ans.org/pi/students/scholarships

American Physical Society (APS)
www.aps.org/programs/honors/other.cfm

American Society for Metals (ASM)
http://asmcommunity.asminternational.
org/portal/site/asm/Home/Foundation

American Society for Nondestructive Testing (ASNT)
asnt.org/keydocuments/awards/awards.htm

American Society of Agricultural and Biological Engineers (ASABE)
asabe.org/membership/students/grant1.html

American Society of Heating, Refrigerating, and Air-Conditioning
    Engineers (ASHRAE)
ashrae.org/students/page/704

American Society of Mechanical Engineers (ASME)
asme.org/Education/College/FinancialAid/Scholarships.cfm

American Society of Naval Engineers (ASNE)
navalengineers.org/Scholarship08-09.html

American Society of Plumbing Engineers (ASPE)
aspe.org/new/ASPE_Scholarship/Steele_Scholarship.php

American Society of Safety Engineers (ASSE)
asse.org

American Welding Society–Foundation (AWS)
aws.org/w/a/foundation/index.html?id=H4N7EfSC

Association for Environmental and Engineering Geologists (AEG)
aegweb.org/i4a/pages/index.cfm?pageid=3410

The Institute of Electrical and Electronic Engineers (IEEE)
ieee.org/web/membership/students/scholarshipsawardscontests/SAG_
homepage.html

Institute of Industrial Engineers (IIE)
iienet2.org/Details.aspx?id=857

Instrumentation, Systems, and Automation Society (ISA)
isa.org/Content/NavigationMenu/General_Information/Careers/
Scholarships/Scholarships.htm

International Association of Lighting Designers (IALD)
iald.org/trust/programs.asp

The Minerals, Metals, and Materials Society (TMS)
tms.org/Students/AwardsPrograms/Scholarships.html

National Society of Professional Engineers (NSPE)
www.nspe.org/Education/awardsandscholarships.html

Nuclear Energy Institute (NEI)
nei.org/careersandeducation/educationandresources/scholarships/
universityscholarshipsandfellowshipsinnuclearenergy

SAE Engineering Scholarships
students.sae.org/awdscholar/scholarships

Society for Mining, Metallurgy, and Exploration (SME)
www.smenet.org/scholarships/

Society of Manufacturing Engineers (SME)
sme.org/cgi-bin/smeefhtml.pl?/foundation/scholarships/fsfstudp
.htm&&&SEF&

Society of Naval Architects and Marine Engineers (SNAME)
sname.org/membership/Scholar.html

Society of Petroleum Engineers (SPE)
spe.org/spe-app/jsp/siteFunctionality/scholarships.jsp

Society of Plastics Engineers (SPE)
www.4spe.org/

SPIE—International Society for Optical Engineering
spie.org/x1733.xml

Technical Association of the Pulp and Paper Industry (TAPPI)
tappi.org/s_tappi/sec.asp?CID=6101&DID=546695

WOMEN AND MINORITIES IN ENGINEERING SCHOLARSHIPS

American Indian Science and Engineering Society (AISES)
www.aises.org/Programs/ScholarshipsandInternships/Scholarships

Diversity Engineering Scholarship Program
engr.utk.edu/desp
University of Tennessee program aimed at African-Americans—allied
with the cooperative engineering program

National Society of Black Engineers (NSBE)
http://national.nsbe.org/Programs/Scholarships/tabid/84/Default.aspx

Society of Hispanic Professional Engineers (SHPE)
shpe.org

Society of Women Engineers (SWE)
swe.org/stellent/idcplg?IdcService=SS_GET_PAGE&nodeId=9&ss
SourceNodeId=5

MISCELLANEOUS SCHOLARSHIPS

Scholarship News is nonengineering specific and includes minority and
engineering scholarship links.
free-4u.com/minority.htm

FREE ONLINE SCHOLARSHIP SEARCH SERVICES

Absolutely Scholarships
scholaraid.com

College Board Online
collegeboard.org

CollegeNET
collegenet.com

FastWeb
fastweb.com

GoCollege
gocollege.com

Sallie Mae College Answer
collegeanswer.com/index.jsp

A P P E N D I X

D

ABET MEMBER SOCIETIES AND DISCIPLINES

American Academy of Environmental Engineers (AAEE)
130 Holiday Court, Suite 100
Annapolis, MD 21404
aaee.net
    Environmental engineering
    Environmental engineering technology

American Congress on Surveying and Mapping (ACSM)
6 Montgomery Village Ave., Suite 403
Gaithersburg, MD 20879
acsm.net
    Surveying
    Surveying engineering
    Survey engineering technology

American Industrial Hygiene Association (AIHA)
2700 Prosperity Ave., Suite 250
Fairfax, VA 22031
aiha.org
    Industrial hygiene

American Institute of Aeronautics and Astronautics (AIAA)
1801 Alexander Bell Dr.
Reston, VA 20191
aiaa.org
    Aerospace engineering
    Aerospace engineering technology

American Institute of Chemical Engineers (AIChE)
Three Park Ave.
New York, NY 10016
aiche.org
    Chemical engineering
    Chemical engineering technology

American Nuclear Society (ANS)
555 N. Kensington Ave.
La Grange Park, IL 60525
ans.org
    Nuclear engineering
    Nuclear engineering technology

American Society for Engineering Education (ASEE)
1818 North St. NW, Suite 600
Washington, DC 20036
asee.org
    Engineering physics
    General engineering
    General engineering technology

American Society of Agricultural and Biological Engineers (ASABE)
2950 Niles Road
St. Joseph, MI 49085
http://asae.org
    Agricultural engineering
    Agricultural engineering technology
    Biological engineering
    Forest engineering

American Society of Civil Engineers (ASCE)
1801 Alexander Bell Dr.
Reston, VA 20191
asce.org
    Architectural engineering
    Architectural engineering technology
    Civil engineering
    Civil engineering technology
    Construction engineering
    Construction engineering technology

American Society of Heating, Refrigerating and Air-Conditioning
    Engineers (ASHRAE)
1791 Tullie Circle NE
Atlanta, GA 30329
ashrae.org
    Air-conditioning engineering
    Air-conditioning engineering technology

American Society of Safety Engineers (ASSE)
1800 E. Oakton St.
Des Plaines, IL 60018
asse.org
    Safety

American Society of Mechanical Engineers (ASME)
Three Park Ave.
New York, NY 10016
asme.org
    Drafting/design engineering technology (mechanical)
    Engineering mechanics
    Mechanical engineering
    Mechanical engineering technology

Biomedical Engineering Society (BMES)
8401 Corporate Dr., Suite 140
Landover, MD 20785
bmes.org
  Bioengineering and biomedical engineering
  Bioengineering technology

Computing Science Accreditation Board (CSAB), Inc.
184 North St.
Stamford, CT 06901
csab.org
  Computer science
  Information systems
  Software engineering

Health Physics Society (HPS)
1313 Dolley Madison Blvd., Suite 402
McLean, VA 22101
hps.org

IEEE, Inc.
IEEE Service Center
445 Hoes Lane
P.O. Box 1331
Piscataway, NJ 08855
ieee.org
  Computer engineering
  Computer engineering technology
  Electrical and electronics engineering
  Electrical and electronics engineering technology
  Telecommunications engineering technology

Institute of Industrial Engineers
25 Technology Park/Atlanta
Norcross, GA 30092
iienet.org

Engineering management
Industrial engineering
Industrial engineering technology
Industrial management

Instrument Society of America (ISA)
67 Alexander Dr.
P.O. Box 12277
Research Triangle Park, NC 27709
isa.org
Instrumentation engineering technology

The Minerals, Metals, and Materials Society (TMS)
184 Thorn Hill Road
Warrendale, PA 15086
tms.org
Materials engineering
Metallurgical engineering
Metallurgical engineering technology
Welding engineering
Welding engineering technology

National Council of Examiners for Engineering and Surveying (NCEES)
P.O. Box 1686
Clemson, SC 29633
ncees.org

National Institute of Ceramic Engineers (NICE)
Department of Materials Science Engineering
P.O. Box 116400
Gainesville, FL 32611
ceramics.org
Ceramic engineering
Ceramic engineering technology

National Society of Professional Engineers (NSPE)
1420 King St.
Alexandria, VA 22314
nspe.org

Society for Mining, Metallurgy, and Exploration, Inc. (SME-AIME)
8307 Shaffer Parkway
P.O. Box 625002
Littleton, CO 80162
smenet.org
  Geological/geophysical engineering
  Mineral engineering
  Mining engineering
  Mining engineering technology

Society of Automotive Engineers (SAE)
400 Commonwealth Dr.
Warrendale, PA 15096
sae.org
  Automotive engineering
  Automotive engineering technology

Society of Manufacturing Engineers (SME)
One SME Dr.
P.O. Box 930
Dearborn, MI 48121
sme.org
  Manufacturing engineering
  Manufacturing engineering technology

Society of Naval Architects and Marine Engineers (SNAME)
601 Pavonia Ave.
Jersey City, NJ 07306
sname.org
  Marine engineering technology
  Naval architecture and marine engineering
  Ocean engineering

Society of Petroleum Engineers (SPE)
P.O. Box 833836
Richardson, TX 75083
spe.org
　　Petroleum engineering
　　Petroleum engineering technology

Materials Research Society (MRS)
9800 McKnight Road
Pittsburgh, PA 15237
mrs.org

ABOUT THE AUTHOR

Dr. Geraldine Garner is the President of Science and Technology Career Strategies, Inc. (STCS, Inc.), which works with companies concerned about retaining key engineering, scientific, and information technology/computer talent. Garner began her career as a co-op coordinator for mechanical and biomedical engineering students at Virginia Tech. Later she became Associate Dean and Associate Professor of the Walter P. Murphy Cooperative Engineering Education Program in the Robert R. McCormick School of Engineering at Northwestern University. She has taught graduate and undergraduate courses in career development theory at Northwestern University and Virginia Commonwealth University.

Garner holds a doctorate in career counseling from Virginia Tech and bachelor's and master's degrees from the College of William and Mary. She is the author of a variety of books, articles, and papers and has received numerous honors for her work with engineers' career development.